# THE D
# KENNEDY
# DIED

# THE DAY

# KENNEDY DIED

## A SNAPSHOT OF THE SIXTIES

Reg Grant

# CONTENTS



*Front cover top left:* Martin Luther King.
*Front cover centre left:* The Beatles.
*Front cover bottom left:* Richard Burton in 'Cleopatra'.
*Front cover centre right and pp2/3:* Dallas on 22 November 1963: Kennedy's car carries the fatally wounded president from the scene of the assassination towards the Parkland Hospital.

*Opposite and front cover bottom:* President and Jacqueline Kennedy smile cheerfully to the crowd. Moments later the assassin's bullets were to rip the president's head apart.

*Back cover and page 1:* All over the world on 23 November 1963 the newspaper headlines were dominated by the news from Dallas.
*All from the Hulton-Deutsch Collection Ltd*


## ACKNOWLEDGEMENTS

The historic newspapers were supplied by the John Frost Historical Newspaper Service. The lines of Philip Larkin's poem 'Annus Mirabilis' published by Faber & Faber in *High Windows* are reproduced by courtesy of the publishers. The lines from Frederick Forsyth's *The Odessa File* are reproduced by courtesy of Random House UK Ltd.

First published 1993

ISBN 0 7110 2191 0





Designed by R.C. Wilcockson

Published by Dial Press

an imprint of Ian Allan Ltd, Terminal House, Station Approach, Shepperton, Surrey TW17 8AS; and printed by Ian Allan Printing Ltd, Coombelands House, Coombelands Lane, Addlestone, Weybridge, Surrey KT15 1HY.

# 1

# PRELUDE

At 7.30 on the morning of 22 November 1963, President John F. Kennedy was woken by his valet in Suite 850 at the Hotel Texas in Fort Worth. The first news of the morning was bad: it was raining, inauspicious weather for a day devoted to showing the President to his people. The crowd already gathering outside the hotel was getting wet, and it seemed the open-top motorcade planned for Dallas at noon might prove impractical. Kennedy was always reluctant to have the bubbletop raised on the custom-built presidential Lincoln. Motorcades had become an important part of electioneering. The slower the motorcade progressed, and the closer and clearer the view people had of the President, the more gratified they were — and the more likely to be influenced to vote for him.

Kennedy was on the second day of a two-day tour of Texas that was crucial to his future political prospects. The state had 24 electoral votes to offer in the 1964 presidential election, which promised to be a close contest. Kennedy was in Texas to reunite his own Democrats — the local party was divided between the liberal Senator Ralph Yarborough and the more conservative Governor John Connally and Vice President Lyndon B. Johnson — and to drum up some personal popularity by smiling and waving at as many people as possible.

With the President at the Hotel Texas, in the second bedroom of the suite, was his wife Jacqueline. She had not previously accompanied her husband on campaigning trips, but it had been felt that her presence in Texas might be an asset. Kennedy was not well liked in the state, and there was the risk of a lukewarm reception that would create an unfavourable impression. The glamour of Jackie was calculated to excite interest and enthusiasm, even among the politically apathetic. Her presence would pull the crowds.

After a light breakfast, the President dressed: an elegant blue-grey suit, a blue tie, and a Parisian Cardin shirt. He was briefed by the CIA on the world situation, including the latest casualty figures from Vietnam (on average, about one American a week was dying in action in Southeast Asia), and then skimmed the newspapers. The reports of his Texan tour were not wholly encouraging. The *New York Times,* for example, under a heading 'Kennedy Pledges Space Advances; Opens Texas Tour' recorded the spirited defence the President had made of the space programme and the large crowds that had greeted his motorcade in San Antonio. But it also homed in on the split in the Texan Democrat party that Kennedy's presence had failed to heal. 'Yarborough Scores Connally,' it headlined, 'and Refuses to Accompany Johnson on Motorcade'.

By the time the President emerged from the hotel to address the crowd outside, he had shrugged off any ill-humour the press reports may have caused. He shunned a raincoat although drizzle was still falling — a macho disdain for minor physical hardships was part of the charismatic Kennedy image — and made a rousing speech of standard political exhortation, concluding 'We are going forward!'. Asked where Jackie was, he replied: 'Mrs Kennedy is organizing herself. It takes her a little longer but, of course, she looks better than we do when she does it.'

There followed a formal breakfast with 2,000 guests, for which Jackie at last turned up to rapturous applause, stylishly late, dressed in a pink suit, pillbox hat, and short white gloves. Presents were given: Texan boots for Jackie, a five-gallon hat for the President. After another speech, the Kennedys had an hour of relative relaxation before their motorcade was to progress to the airport for the short flight to Dallas.

During this interlude the President's political adviser Ken O'Donnell drew his attention to an item in the *Dallas Morning News* that day. In a full-page advertisement ironically entitled 'Welcome Mr Kennedy', local right-wingers launched a wildly inaccurate, scabrous attack on the President's allegedly pro-communist policies. This broadside followed the distribution of handbills in Dallas the previous day showing Kennedy full face and profile, with the headline WANTED FOR TREASON. For Kennedy, reading the *Dallas Morning News* advertisement sparked off a dramatic fantasy. Turning to Jackie, he said: 'You know, last night would have been a hell of a night to assassinate a President.'

In 1963, Dallas was a boom city with a population already topping three-quarters of a million and rising fast. Its civic leaders were eager to shake off an old reputation as the 'hate capital of Dixie'. They prided themselves on a new civic image of cleanliness and culture — the city had its

**The Kennedy era witnessed the dawn of the manned space race. Here, President John F. Kennedy (left) and Vice-President Lyndon B. Johnson (right) flank Lt-Col John H. Glenn — the first American in space — on 24 February 1962.**
***The Hulton-Deutsch Collection Ltd***

***Right:*** **Keeping it in the family: President Kennedy's Attorney General was his younger brother Robert. Ironically, Robert Kennedy himself was to be assassinated in 1968 whilst campaigning to become Democratic presidential candidate. *The Hulton-Deutsch Collection Ltd***

"All the News That's Fit to Print"

# The New York Times.

LATE CITY EDITION
U. S. Weather Bureau Report (Page 74) forecast: Sunny, warm today and tomorrow. Clear and mild tonight.
Temp. Range: 67—50; yesterday: 56—48.

VOL. CXIII . . No. 38,653. © 1963 by The New York Times Company. Times Square, New York 36, N. Y. | NEW YORK, FRIDAY, NOVEMBER 22, 1963. | TEN CENTS

## KENNEDY PLEDGES SPACE ADVANCES; OPENS TEXAS TOUR

Dedicates San Antonio Site and Declares Research 'Must and Will Go On'

PARTY SPLIT EVIDENCED

Yarborough Scores Connally and Refuses to Accompany Johnson on Motorcade

By TOM WICKER
Special to The New York Times

HOUSTON, Nov. 21—President Kennedy mixed a strong defense of his space program with some old-fashioned, earth-bound politics today as he opened a two-day tour of Texas.

In this space-conscious state, he pledged that the conquest of that "new frontier" would go ahead.

He gave the reassurance despite Congressional reductions in his space budget.

He declared in a speech at Brooks Air Force Base:

"There will be setbacks and frustrations and disappointments. There will be pressures for our country to do less and temptations to do something else. But this research must and will go on. The conquest of space must and will go ahead. That much we know. That much we can say with confidence and conviction."

Cheered by Crowds

The President was welcomed by large crowds lining the streets of San Antonio and Houston as he and Mrs. Kennedy drove past in an open car.

His San Antonio motorcade took him from the city's International Airport to the new Aero-Space Medical Health Center at the nearby air base.

After he helped dedicate a new $6 million facility there he [illegible]

DISCUSS PARTY UNITY: Gov. William W. Scranton of Pennsylvania and Governor Rockefeller at news conference, held in Mr. Rockefeller's office, 22 West 55th Street. *The New York Times*

## BYRNES DEFENDS STOCK PURCHASE

Denies Wrongdoing in Deal With Company He Aided—Will Give Away Profit

By EILEEN SHANAHAN
Special to The New York Times

WASHINGTON, Nov. 21—Representative John W. Byrnes sought today, with apparent success, to convince his Congressional colleagues that he had done nothing wrong by buying stock at a reduced rate from a company for which he had obtained a favorable tax ruling.

Republicans in the House of Representatives, then all except [illegible]

## Rockefeller to Avoid Pennsylvania Drive For Delegates Now

By BERNARD STENGREN

Governor Rockefeller agreed yesterday that the need for Republican party unity in Pennsylvania took precedence now over his quest for delegate votes at the party's Presidential nominating convention next year.

At an 80-minute meeting in his office here at 22 West 55th Street with Gov. William W. Scranton of Pennsylvania, Mr. Rockefeller promised that he would not attempt to seek commitments from Pennsylvania's 64 delegates "without consulting and agreeing with Governor Scranton."

The two Governors disclosed this at a news conference following the meeting.

## LOST SOYBEAN OIL PUZZLES WALL ST.

Exporter Charges That Tons of Commodity Are Missing —Stock Prices Plunge

By H. J. MAIDENBERG

The alleged disappearance of millions of pounds of soybean oil has added to Wall Street's biggest mystery of the year.

The story involves two prominent brokerage houses suspended from the major stock exchanges and the filing for bankruptcy of a vegetable-oil refining company. Caught in the squeeze are thousands of private investors.

Yesterday, the Bunge Corporation, a major commodities ex- [illegible]

## COUNCIL APPROVES NON-LATIN FORMS FOR SACRAMENTS

Authorizes Bishops to Use Vernacular—Statement on Jews Is Put Off

By MILTON BRACKER
Special to The New York Times

ROME, Nov. 21—The Ecumenical Council authorized today the use of vernacular languages—English in the United States—for the Roman Catholic sacraments.

The move included even the essential key phrase of each sacrament. By an earlier vote, this was to be retained in Latin.

For example, when the latest decision is fully implemented, the phrase "Ego te absolvo a peccatis tuis in nomine Patris et Filii et Spiritus Sancti" in the sacrament of penance may be spoken by the priest in English. ("I absolve thee from thy sins in the name of the Father and of the Son and of the Holy Spirit.")

Move on Unity Advanced

The latest victory for liturgical reform—expected to be the first subject formally promulgated by the Council, at a public or plenary session next Friday—came on a day of other important procedural developments. These included:

¶Council approval of the first three chapters of the schema on ecumenism, or the movement toward unity among Christians, as a basis for discussion.

¶Announcement by the moderators or rotating chairmen that separate votes would be taken at an unspecified date on Chapters 4 and 5. These deal respectively with the relations between Roman Catholics and Jews, and with religious liberty.

While it was emphasized that this change did not constitute a "scuttling" of the two chapters, as one churchman strongly favorable to them put it, it was acknowledged that there was a possibility that the votes on [illegible]

## Congo Ousts Soviet Aides; Suspends Ties to Moscow

*Entire Embassy Staff Is Told to Leave —Adoula Asserts Diplomats Sought to Undermine His Regime*

By Reuters

LEOPOLDVILLE, the Congo, Nov. 21—The Congolese Government in effect suspended diplomatic relations with the Soviet Union today. It ordered the expulsion of the entire 100-member staff of the Soviet Embassy, including the two diplomats who were arrested Tuesday.

An official Congolese announcement said the two diplomats and another Russian who was arrested, a correspondent of the Soviet press agency Novosty, were released this afternoon. The two diplomats were ordered to leave within 48 hours.

Premier Cyrille Adoula said at a press conference that documents found in the possession of the two Russians proved that they were working with a "National Liberation Committee" formed in Brazzaville by Christophe Gbenye, who was a supporter of the late Patrice Lumumba.

Mr. Lumumba was the first Premier of the Congo and his regime was strongly supported by the Soviet Union.

Mr. Adoula said that among the documents found on the Soviet diplomats was a letter from Mr. Gbenye's committee to a member of the Soviet Embassy in Leopoldville asking for 5 billion Congolese francs (about $29,400) in forged bills, arms, tape recorders and other equipment.

"All these documents prove irrefutably the collusion of the Soviet Embassy in the Congo with this committee, composed of a handful of Congolese agitators who style themselves a

Continued on Page 11, Column 1

## Erhard, in Paris, Stresses Benefits of Link With U.S.

By DREW MIDDLETON
Special to The New York Times

PARIS, Nov. 21—Dr. Ludwig Erhard, West Germany's new Chancellor, arrived in the French capital today proclaiming that a close Atlantic partnership was valuable to both France and West Germany.

This allusion to West Germany's interest in maintaining intimate ties with the United States as well as with France was expected by diplomats to set the tone for the Chancellor's talks with President de Gaulle.

The meeting with General de Gaulle is Dr. Erhard's first since he succeeded Dr. Konrad Adenauer.

The French President and his guest met privately for 90 min- [illegible]

## U. S. SCALES DOWN HELP TO INDONESIA

Shipments of Plane Parts Halted to Prod Sukarno on Malaysia Issue

By M. S. HANDLER

## CAMBODIA URGES PARIS TO REPLACE REJECTED U.S. AID

Surprise Request Is Studied by French—They Extend Trade Tie With Hanoi

BID BY DE GAULLE SEEN

He Is Again Expected to Seek Influence in Asia—China Pledges Help to Prince

By PETER GROSE
Special to The New York Times

PARIS, Nov. 21—Prince Norodom Sihanouk of Cambodia has requested French economic aid to replace the United States assistance program canceled yesterday. The request was being studied today by the French Government.

French officials also disclosed today the renewal of a commercial agreement with North Vietnam. There were indications that the establishment of formal diplomatic relations between Paris and the Communist regime in Hanoi would soon follow.

[The official press agency of the Peking Government said that Communist China had pledged "all-out support" for Cambodia in the event of an "armed invasion instigated by the United States and its vassals." Prince Sihanouk, according to a Reuters report, proposed a 14-nation conference to guarantee the neutrality of Cambodia.]

French Bid Expected

The request from the Prince and the renewal of ties with Hanoi open the way for a new bid for influence in Southeast Asia by President de Gaulle. His policy for a reunited and neutral Vietnam was apparently checked by this month's military coup in Saigon.

Prince Sihanouk's request for French assistance was disclosed

***Below:*** **The headline from *The New York Times* for 22 November highlighted Kennedy's promise to maintain the space programme at the start of his tour to Texas. Other news that day included a report from Rome that the Ecumenical Council had authorised the use of vernacular languages — rather than Latin — in Roman Catholic sacraments. In the event all the day's news was to be overshadowed by the reports from Dallas.**

symphony orchestra, its opera, its arts museum. But many of Dallas's citizens expressed values and attitudes that still reflected the suspicion, narrowness and prejudice of traditional Southern white society. The city was a violent place: in 1963, up to 22 November, it had been the scene of 110 murders (more than double the number of Americans who had been killed that year in Vietnam). Most of the deaths had been by firearms since there were no gun laws at all.

Dallas was notorious as a stronghold of right-wing extremism. It was a centre of hostility to Kennedy's liberal policies on race and his allegedly soft line on communism. A substantial section of the population felt a genuine hatred for the President. They had an all-white society's deep-rooted fear of racial equality, a fundamentalist protestantism that rejected Kennedy's tolerance of diversity as 'anti-Christian', and a disgust at the 'subversives, perverts, and miscellaneous security risks' that, according to one of the city's newspapers, made up the majority of the 'pinko' Kennedy administration.

There had been repeated warnings that the city was not a safe place for Kennedy to visit. A leading Texan Democrat, Byron Skelton, had written to Robert Kennedy to say he would 'feel better if the President's itinerary did not include

Dallas'. The liberal Senator J. William Fulbright had told Kennedy more than a month before the visit that 'Dallas is a very dangerous place. I wouldn't go there. Don't you go.'

Even the individuals who delivered these warnings, however, were probably thinking more in terms of an unpleasant incident than an actual attempt on the President's life. No American head of state had been assassinated since President William McKinley in 1901. But Adlai Stevenson, then US Ambassador to the UN, had been jeered and spat upon by a hostile crowd during a visit to Dallas on 24 October. The city authorities were keen to prevent a similar incident occurring during Kennedy's visit and passed a special city ordinance giving them powers to crack down on hostile demonstrations. Although only a minority of its citizens were wholeheartedly looking forward to the Kennedy visit, 22 November was not quite a day like any other for Dallas. As well as carrying the scurrilous 'Welcome Mr President' advertisement, the *Dallas Morning News* appeared with details of the route and timing of the motorcade — which had

**The start of a tragic day: President and Mrs Jacqueline Kennedy are greeted at Dallas airport. Standing behind them is the Texas Governor, John B. Connally. Connally, too, was to be hit during the fateful cavalcade through the streets of Dallas.** ***The Hulton-Deutsch Collection Ltd***

already been published some days before — and the comment that 'the motorcade will move slowly so that crowds can "get a good view" of President Kennedy and his wife.' Many citizens intended to do just that.

Another city might have declared a school holiday for a presidential visit, but in Dallas it was business as usual. Children were only permitted to go see the President if their parents came to collect them, and some teachers forbade it even then, taking the opportunity to inform their pupils of Kennedy's iniquities. But the motorcade was timed to pass through the city centre at lunchtime, so office workers would have an unusual entertainment for their break. The local Kennedy supporters and anti-Kennedy protesters would, of course, be out in force, but so would the plain curious. One man intending to see the parade was a dress manufacturer, Abraham Zapruder. As an afterthought, at the time when Kennedy was addressing the crowds outside Hotel Texas, Zapruder went home from his business premises to pick up his movie camera.

The knowledge that there might be

**Little knowing what was to befall them, the members presidential group look relaxed as it prepares to depart. *The Hulton-Deutsch Collection Ltd***

## GUNNING FOR KENNEDY

If the President had had copies of the British popular newspapers to read on the morning of 22 November, he might have paused at a headline in the *Daily Express*. Across the full width of page 11 it read: 'THE MAN WHO'S GUNNING FOR KENNEDY'. Underneath was a photo of an elderly individual in a stetson posed with a rifle: the right-wing Senator Barry Goldwater, Kennedy's most likely Republican opponent in the forthcoming presidential election.

Another coincidental premonition was contained in the non-fiction bestseller list in the current edition of *Time* magazine. Top of the list stood *JFK: The Man and the Myth*; directly below it, *The American Way of Death*.

If these coincidences seemed to foreshadow the assassination, no such foresight was vouchsafed to the practitioners of the science of astrology. Maurice Woodruff, probably the most prestigious astrologer of the day, cast the President's horoscope just over a week before the assassination. Under 'pointers for your year ahead' he informed Kennedy that the future would not be 'quiet or restful' but that 1964 would see him re-elected by a narrow majority, and that his wife could look forward to another pregnancy by the year's end.

PHOTO NEWS EXTRA ...PRESENTING CRACKSHOT GOLDWATER—PICTURED BY KARSH

**The man who's gunning for Kennedy**

Goldwater in uniform of simple Westerner: Stetson, jeans, stained jacket, rifle. Cactus background, however, is not in his native Arizona desert but in a garden...

Barry Goldwater, business man—in dark suit, white shirt, sober tie

trouble also added to the atmosphere. Just after 8 o'clock on the morning of 22 November, Dallas citizens who tuned into NBC's *Today* show could see their Police Chief, Jesse Curry, describing the precautions he had put in place and warning that action would be taken against anyone who caused a disturbance during the President's visit. Expectations of an incident were high.

By the time Kennedy and his entourage landed at Love Field, Dallas, after the 13-minute hop from Fort Worth, the weather had cleared. The sun was shining, although there were still puddles on the tarmac. It was 11.25 a.m. An enthusiastic crowd of local Kennedy supporters had gathered at the airport, and the President strolled across to shake hands with his public and proffer his dazzling smile at closer range — shadowed at all times by his watchful secret service bodyguard.

The motorcade finally moved out of the airport at 11.55 a.m. In the presidential car with Kennedy and Jacqueline were the driver, Bill Greer, Roy Kellerman of the Secret Service, and Governor Connally and his wife. It was hot as the cars processed through the outskirts of Dallas. The sun blazed down upon the half-empty sidewalks of light industrial zones and residential suburbs. Kennedy stopped the car twice, to shake hands with a group of children and to talk to a bevy of nuns. The priorities of electioneering made such actions a conditioned reflex - no security considerations could have prevented a president responding to these stimuli in this way.

As the motorocade advanced into the centre of Dallas, the crowd lining the route thickened. On Main Street, cheering, waving onlookers were ten-deep on the sidewalks and hanging out of office windows. The President and Jackie smiled and waved back to the crowd, trying to give as many people as possible that special feeling — that these famous and powerful individuals had smiled and waved at *them*

**Back in Britain, the *Daily Express* of 22 November carried a feature on Senator Barry Goldwater, later the Republican candidate for the presidency in 1964, under the headline 'The man who's gunning for Kennedy'. Twenty-four hours later the *Daily Express*, and the rest of Fleet Street, would be recording the actual assassination.**

**With flags fluttering, the Presidential motorcade passes through downtown Dallas. Moments later the gunman was to strike, fatally wounding Kennedy and severely injuring Connally by his side.** ***The Hulton-Deutsch Collection Ltd***

in person. After all the gloomy and nervous prognostications, it was a triumphant show. In the heart of enemy territory, Kennedy was winning an impressive reception.

The final destination of the motorcade was the Dallas Trade Mart, where the President was to speak at lunch. To reach this destination, the procession had to turn right off Main Street at Houston Street, and then immediately left onto Elm Street. At the intersection of Houston and Elm was a brick-built warehouse, the Texas School Book Depository.

On Houston the crowds were thinner, but still enthusiastic. The motorcade would soon be out of the city centre, and the participants started to relax. Mrs Connally turned to the President and commented: 'You sure can't say Dallas doesn't love you, Mr President.' 'No, you can't,' he replied.

The turn onto Elm Street was sharp and slowed the cars to a crawl. The President's vehicle moved forward under the windows of the Book Depository at precisely 11.2 miles per hour. The President raised his hand to wave to a young boy held up above the crowd. The time was 12.30.

## Welcome Mr Kennedy

Copies of the *Dallas Morning News* on 22 November carried a full-page advertisement, surrounded by a funereal black border, headed 'WELCOME MR KENNEDY'. Attributed to The American Fact Finding Committee, 'An unaffiliated and non-partisan group of citizens who wish the truth', the advert was a virulent attack on the President's policies.

The 'free-thinking and America-thinking citizens of Dallas' behind the advertisement posed Kennedy a series of hostile questions, including:

'WHY do you say we have built a wall of freedom around Cuba when there is no freedom in Cuba today...?

'WHY did you host, salute and entertain Tito — Moscow's Trojan Horse — just a short time after our sworm enemy, Khrushchev, embraced the Yugoslav dictator as a great hero and leader of Communism?

'WHY has Gus Hall, head of the US Communist Party, praised almost every one of your policies...?

'WHY have you ordered or permitted your brother Bobby, the Attorney General, to go soft on Communists, fellow-travelers, and ultra-leftists in America, while permitting him to persecute loyal Americans who criticize you, your administration, and your leadership?'

The diatribe concluded: 'MR KENNEDY, as citizens of these United States of America, we DEMAND answers to these questions, and we want them NOW.'

**The American south had been a hotbed of racial tension in the period leading up to Kennedy's visit. Typical of the propaganda of the era was this billboard purporting to show civil rights leader Martin Luther King at a Communist training school. King, himself assassinated in 1968, vehemently denied the allegations.**
***The Hulton-Deutsch Collection Ltd***

# 2

# A LOST WORLD

Assassinations often enter historical mythology as a moment when a world lost its innocence. It is tempting to see the rifle shots that cracked across Dealey Plaza on 22 November 1963 as wakening a fresh and uncorrupted world to a vicious and disillusioning reality. So many of the memorable icons of the day — the early Beatles, the Kennedys, Mary Quant fashions, 'Blowin' in the Wind', Pop Art — seem retrospectively to spell out a message of fresh, youthful optimism.

Many Americans were later to look back on the Kennedy era as a time of peace, strength and liberal righteousness, and to see what followed as moral collapse and national humiliation: race riots; defeat in the Vietnam War; the assassination of the heroes of liberalism and civil rights; Watergate. Disc jockey Paul Gambuccini, a high school pupil in Connecticut when the assassination took place, spoke for many Americans who were young at that time when he said: 'This was the great watershed of our lives. Before Kennedy's killing we were patriots. After 1963, we noticed more and more of the dark side of our country's character...'

Most of the British population apparently also sees the early 1960s as a halcyon era. According to a Gallup Poll conducted in Britain in 1993, about four out of five respondents asserted that 30 years ago life had been better than today: a time when there had been no need to fortify your house against burglars, you could walk the streets safely at night, people were kind and considerate, the British bobby was the best policeman in the world, the countryside was unspoilt, children were usually well behaved and the British health and education systems were something to be proud of.

The reality, of course, in Britain, the United States and elsewhere, was to say the least more mixed. The world of the Kennedy presidency was, for example, one in which blacks through large areas of the United States were denied the right to vote; in Britain, many pubs and clubs banned black customers and a by-election at Smethwick, Birmingham, was fought with the slogan: 'If you want a nigger for a neighbour, vote Labour.' It was a world in which all homosexual relationships were against the law; for unmarried women, contraception was almost impossible to procure and pregnancy brought shame and, often, rejection by her family; and abortions were performed illegally, often under insanitary conditions by individuals of dubious medical standing. It was a world gripped by a nuclear arms race between the United States and the Soviet Union that threatened universal catastrophe, the world of Dr Strangelove in which sane American leaders embraced the doctrine of MAD: Mutually Assured Destruction. And it was a world in which democracy and human rights were rare flowers among the weeds of dictatorship, imperialism and totalitarianism that flourished across the globe.

***Above:*** **The civil rights movement in the United States was one of the great popular campaigns of the late 20th century, eventually forcing a reluctant white majority to concede reforms that radically altered the position of the black minority in the country. Three months before the death of Kennedy, on 28 August 1963, the march on Washington organised by the National Association for the Advancement of Colored People culminated with a demonstration along Constitution Avenue in Washington.** ***The Hulton-Deutsch Collection Ltd***

***Left:*** **Racism was also an issue in Britain. In 1963 employees of the Bank of India picketed the company's Moorgate offices after the bank dismissed an Indian member of staff for attempting to organise a trade union branch.** ***The Hulton-Deutsch Collection Ltd***

On the other side of the coin, in 1963 there was no AIDS and no international terrorism. The abuse of hard drugs was the habit of a tiny minority and the incidence of crime, although alarming to contemporaries, was less than one fifth of the level of the early 1990s. In so many places that have since been devastated by war and anarchy — Northern Ireland, Lebanon, Cambodia, Afghanistan, much of Africa, the former Yugoslavia and Soviet Union — an orderly and secure everyday life was possible, even if scarred by poverty, corruption or oppression.

The Earth was strikingly less crowded in 1963, with a population that had just passed 3 billion, around half the figure for the 1990s. And in the developed countries, it was certainly a younger world than today. In Britain one quarter of the population was under 15 years old, and in the United States the comparable figure was almost one third, as the baby boom of the immediate postwar period fed through into adolescence.

If there was one point on which all cultural commentators agreed, it was that the 1960s would be the decade of youth. Kennedy, at 43 the youngest US president ever elected, with his even younger brother Robert as attorney general, had made an appeal to youthful idealism one of the themes of his administration. There was a sense that the old guard from the war years, those stiff father figures with their medals and uniforms — General Eisenhower, General de Gaulle, Marshal Tito, Generalissimo Franco were destined to give way before new energies and purposes.

At a more mundane level, full employment meant young people had money in their pockets and no fear for the future. As commerce identified 'youth' as a market, so young people identified themselves self-consciously as the collective proprietors of this 'youth', a valuable commodity not to be squandered on preparation for the grey dimness of adulthood, but to be savoured for its own sake. There was a widespread revolt against the narrow perspectives of an older generation that had been shaped by the cumulative experiences of depression, war and austerity. The teenagers of 1963 could not remember the war even as a childhood experience — except as ever-present in comics and films. In Britain, National Service was at an end and splashes of colour were appearing in the limited provincial society so well portrayed by the British cinema of the

**KENNEDY AND THE 'OLD MEN': 1**
**Present Kennedy greets Britain's Prime Minister, Harold MacMillan, at Washington Airport on 29 April 1962.*The Hulton-Deutsch Collection Ltd***

**KENNEDY AND THE 'OLD MEN': 2**
**In May 1963 Kennedy visited French president, General Charles de Gaulle.**
***The Hulton-Deutsch Collection Ltd***

time (*Saturday Night, Sunday Morning,* or *Billy Liar*).

The Western world was in the middle of the biggest economic boom in history, which since 1950 had raised the living standards of the general population at a rate never accomplished before or since. Through the vehicle of Keynsian economics the major nations had achieved the miracle of endless growth and full employment. In Britain 474,317 people were unemployed, about 2 percent of the workforce — and this figure was shocking enough to create a sense of economic crisis. (In the early 1990s unemployment never fell below 8 percent of the workforce.) Inflation also stood at 2 percent a year, another figure considered offensively high at the time. Most economic experts were agreed what should be done: Britain needed more state planning, less capitalist laissez-faire. Although stark poverty existed in all Western countries, progress toward equality was almost universally recognized as an ideal. With every year that passed, the gap between the rich and the middle income class narrowed, and so did the gap between the middle incomes and the poor.

The new consumer goods that had transformed domestic life in the United States during the 1950s were now marching into more and more British homes. Washing machines and spin driers were transforming the lives of women at home (housework was almost exclusively a female activity), rapidly joining the vacuum cleaner as standard household equipment in Britain. Car ownership was on a sharp upward curve: the Mini, first mass-produced in 1960, seemed a symbol of the new times — popular at all levels of society, efficiently designed for crowded urban living, an image of lightweight fun.

The new comforts and conveniences of life still had some way to go, however. Only one third of British households had a fridge, and one in eight still lacked a television. Central heating was not a standard fitting even in new houses. On the nippy autumn evening of 22 November, most British families were sitting by a hearth of coal or smokeless fuel, a primitive gas fire, a paraffin stove or the bars of an electric heater; for very many women, each

**KENNEDY AND THE 'OLD MEN': 3**
***Right:*** **A month before his death President Kennedy played host to President Tito of Yugoslavia and his wife in Washington. Tito is seen addressing the crowds at the White House on 21 October 1963.** ***The Hulton-Deutsch Collection Ltd***

**KENNEDY AND THE 'OLD MEN': 4**
***Below:*** **The Kennedy family was Irish-American in origin and in June 1963 the President visited the Republic. He is seen with Irish premier Eamonn De Valera at Dublin Airport on 28 June.** ***The Hulton-Deutsch Collection Ltd***

day started with the dirty and laborious business of lighting a fire, kneeling to a pile of wood, paper and coal. Owning a telephone was also still a sign of middle class prosperity — there were nine million phones in Britain — although articles in the newspapers of 22 November proudly promised that, with a new investment programme, telephones would be available for all who wanted them in five years time.

The modern world was arriving in Britain, but much of the old still survived. People bought goods from assistants behind counters, rather than self-service. Sunday night was bath night and Monday was washing day. The last trams were disappearing from Britain's cities, but there were no pedestrian precincts. The brave new world of motorways (the first stretch of the M1 had opened in 1959) and high-rise developments had begun to appear, but the devastation of the Victorian city centres and the old terraced streets was far from complete. *Coronation Street* was half an exercise in gritty contemporary realism, half already a cosy nostalgic reflection on an idealised lost way of life. Audiences could laugh comfortably at *Steptoe and Son* with its hip bath in front of

# A PLACE TO LIVE

In November 1963, you could buy a luxury four-bedroomed town house in London's fashionable St John's Wood area for £18,000. This was very expensive indeed. A similar house in respectably suburban Golders Green was priced at £7,950. Outside London £4,000 or less bought a good family home. But incomes were also staggeringly low by modern standards. The *Sunday Times* carried an advertisement for a Group Personnel Manager, aged 35-48, with a salary of £2,500 to £3,000 a year. A teacher, a graduate chemist or a youth employment officer could expect to earn between £700 and £900 a year.

Housing estates for private ownership were spreading across Britain at a fast pace, cheap boxes for living in, each with its patch of garden and its garage — a new requirement as car ownership spread. About 178,000 houses were built for private sale in 1963, compared with 124,000 built as public housing for the local councils; ten years earlier the balance had been 245,000 council to 65,000 private. Home ownership was still a largely middle class privilege however. Ten million people owned their homes in 1963; by 1992 the figure would be 17 million.

2 THE TIMES FRIDAY NOVEMBER 22 1963

APPOINTMENTS AND SITUATIONS

VACANT and REQUIRED

Imperial Chemical Industries Limited

TECHNICAL OFFICER DEVELOPMENT

BRITISH VISQUEEN LIMITED

The Personnel Officer, British Visqueen Limited, Six Hills Way, Stevenage, Herts.

FISONS LIMITED

MANAGEMENT ACCOUNTANT

O & M OFFICER

PUNCH CARD SUPERVISOR

EUROPEAN ORGANIZATION FOR NUCLEAR RESEARCH GENEVA, SWITZERLAND

GRADUATE PHYSICISTS and ENGINEERS

ASSISTANT TO MANAGING DIRECTOR OF PUBLISHING COMPANY

BIRDS EYE

COMPANY WORK STUDY MANAGER

Managing Director

BRITISH IRON AND STEEL FEDERATION

Intelligence Department

ENGINEERING UNDERGRADUATES

VACANCIES FOR ENGINEERING ASSISTANTS

THE METROPOLITAN WATER BOARD

CIVIL ENGINEERING

MECHANICAL ENGINEERING

ELECTRICAL ENGINEERING

GENERAL WORKS MANAGER

BRAND MANAGEMENT

ASSISTANT WORKS MANAGER

CHIEF ACCOUNTANT

COUNTRY LIFE—NOVEMBER 21, 1963 SUPPLEMENT—11

ESTATE HARRODS OFFICES

KENsington 1490

Telegrams: "Estate, Harrods, London"

32, 34 and 36, HANS CRESCENT, LONDON, S.W.1

West Byfleet

Haslemere and Berkhamsted

**TEDDINGTON**

AN ATTRACTIVE RIVERSIDE HOUSE

FREEHOLD FOR SALE with possession Privately or by Auction December 4

**COLESHILL, AMERSHAM**

A SMALL LUXURY HOUSE OF OUTSTANDING MERIT

£9,950

**WEST CLANDON, SURREY**

EXCEPTIONALLY WELL APPOINTED MODERN HOUSE

FREEHOLD £9,950

**SOUTH CROYDON-PURLEY BORDERS**

ARCHITECT DESIGNED MODERN DETACHED HOUSE OF CHARACTER

standing well back from quiet, tree-lined road

FOR SALE FREEHOLD

**NR. WELWYN, HERTS**

ATTRACTIVE MODERN HOUSE

FREEHOLD £6,950

**FAVOURITE OXTED DISTRICT**

IDEAL COLLEGE-STYLED RESIDENCE

Built on simple lines

1 ACRE

FREEHOLD £9,000

**OUTSKIRTS OF NORTH LONDON**

A QUITE SUPERIOR DETACHED DOUBLE-FRONTED BUNGALOW

FREEHOLD POSSESSION APRIL, 1964

**WALTON HEATH, SURREY**

ONE OF THE FINEST MODERN HOUSES IN THE COUNTY

FREEHOLD

***Above:*** **The appointments page from *The Times* of 22 November 1963. Amongst jobs advertised were posts at the Metropolitan Water Board (with starting salaries of £835pa) and a Managing Director of an anonymous northeastern company at £2,500.**

***Left:*** **Just as salaries were much lower than in the 1990s so too were the prices of desirable country residences. *Country Life* on 21 November 1963 could offer, through Harrods, a four-bedroom house near Welwyn at £6,950 and a modern house at West Clandon at £9,950.**

At lower social levels, house purchase was out of the question. The majority of the population still depended on council housing or the private rented sector. In an article in the *TV Times* in November 1963, a newly-wed clerk described the problems of setting up home in London: 'I clear about £11 10s a week out of £13 and my wife Teen gets about £7 10s clear... A typical pad for rent was two dingy rooms off a communal passage with a chipped sink, a gas ring and no furniture, with four families sharing a toilet. That went for £4 5s.' The average British family was well off compared with its predecessors, at least if both partners were in work, but they could still only afford poor accommodation.

## The space race

Under the Cold War conditions of the early 1960s, it was inevitable that space exploration developed into a contest between the two superpowers, the United States and the Soviet Union, with both national prestige and military objectives at stake. The Soviet Union had won the race to put the first satellite in orbit and the first man in space. On 22 November Valentina Tereshkova, the Soviet astronaut who had become the first woman in space the previous June, was touring India as part of a Soviet propaganda exercise.

The Americans had done their best to reply to the Soviet triumphs, using the power of television: the first US manned space flights, by Alan Shephard and John Glenn, had been broadcast live across America. School children were assembled around portable televisions to watch the events, and the President had himself photographed watching the flights on television at the White House, with his wife and Vice President Lyndon Johnson. (During the countdown for the John Glenn flight, the Vice-President was heard to mutter: 'If only he was a Negro.')

On the day before his assassination, visiting Brooks Air Force Base at San Antonio, Texas, Kennedy delivered a speech in defence of the space programme, threatened

**Two of the world's first cosmonauts — Yuri Gagarin (second from left) and Valentina Nikolayeva Tereshkova (second from right) — are pictured after their triumphs. Gagarin was the first man in space and Tereshkova the first woman.** ***The Hulton-Deutsch Collection Ltd***

## Pop art

Nothing captures the flavour of 1963 quite as effectively as the Pop Art movement which was then at its height. Artists had been expected to reject the vulgarity and tastelessness of popular culture, asserting alternative, 'higher' values. Now here were painters and sculptors who revelled in bad taste and embraced the mass-produced modern world with open arms.

In the United States the main practitioners of Pop Art were Roy Lichtenstein, with his giant-size cartoon frames, the sculptor Claes Oldenburg, who was exhibiting large-scale replicas of hamburgers and ice-cream cones, and Andy Warhol, who had achieved instant notoriety as the man who made art out of soup cans.

On the surface, these works seemed a celebration of Americana, a naïve hymn to the consumer paradise that the United States had become. But the darker side of America in 1963 was also present in Pop Art, especially in Warhol's work. He had moved on from soup cans to silkscreen prints of fatal car crashes, electric chairs and racist police attacking black protestors. These were also Americana, but of a less palatable variety.

In Britain Peter Blake, Richard Hamilton and David Hockney celebrated popular culture in a lighter vein. Hockney, already famous at 25, was only marginally 'Pop' in his art, but quintessentially 'Pop' in his per-

**Although the Russians were the first to send a manned space craft into orbit, the Americans were not far behind. Codenamed 'Project Mercury', the operation made John E. Glenn (second from right on the front row) the first American in space. *The Hulton-Deutsch Collection Ltd***

by Congressional cutbacks. The President, who had promised to put an American on the Moon by the end of the decade, declared:

'This is an era which calls for action, and for the best efforts of all those who would test the unknown and the uncertain in every phase of human endeavour. It is a time for pathfinders and pioneers... There will be setbacks and frustrations and disappointments. There will be pressures for our country to do less and temptations to do something else. But... the conquest of space must and will go ahead... this nation has tossed its cap over the wall of space — and we have no choice but to follow it...'

**Strange art in a strange location: Sir Kenneth Clarke, later to be immortalised through his television series *Civilisation*, opened an exhibition of modern art in a Piccadilly Arcade laundry a few days after Kennedy's death. *The Hulton-Deutsch Collection Ltd***

sonality. He projected a sense of art as fun, a visual excitement that did not have to be weighty or serious.

There was also a new movement in British sculpture, associated with the influence of Anthony Caro, that rejected traditional numinous materials such as stone and wood in favour of metal girders, plastics and fibreglass, often painted in bright, positive colours. The message — or part of it — was that art embraced the present and the future: 'Roll Over Michelangelo'.

## Royalty

In November 1963, the most high-profile member of the British royal family was Princess Margaret, who had taken the popular step of marrying a commoner, photographer Tony Armstrong-Jones, two years earlier. Her son, Viscount Linley, was one year old, and she was pregnant again, with Lady Sarah Armstrong-Jones.

The Queen, then 37 years old, was also pregnant, with Prince Edward. The Prince of Wales was a gawky 15-year-old; his future wife was a two-year-old baby.

The publication of Princess Margaret's husband's intimate photos of his wife with her baby at this time was perhaps the first step in the modern populariza-tion of the 'royals' through emphasising their private lives — a path that would eventually lead to disastrous exposure.

***Above:*** **The youthful Prince Charles, then in his early teens, enjoyed a ski-ing holiday in Switzerland during January 1963. Thirty years on, such a holiday would have, no doubt, inspired much comment amongst the tabloids but, at the time, royalty was treated with much greater deference. *The Hulton-Deutsch Collection Ltd***

***Below:*** **HRH Princess Margaret, Countess Snowdon, and Lord Snowdon admire a Vauxhall Viva at the Motor Show in October 1963. *The Hulton-Deutsch Collection Ltd***

**Roley, the King Charles Spaniel, returned from its summer holiday at Sandringham on 6 August 1963 in the company of Lord Snowdon, Prince Charles and Princess Margaret. *The Hulton-Deutsch Collection Ltd***

**A famous figure who would be unable to comment on where he heard about the death of President Kennedy was Aldous Huxley, the famous British author. *The Hulton-Deutsch Collection Ltd***

## PROPHET OF PSYCHEDELIA

English novelist Aldous Huxley died in Hollywood, California, on the day of the Kennedy assassination. He was 69.

Coming from a family famous for its rationalists and scientists — his grandfather Thomas Huxley had been the most prominent propagandist for Darwin's theory of evolution in the 19th century, Huxley had begun his writing career as a cynical satirist, mirroring the hedonistic decadence of the 1920s. His most famous work, *Brave New World*, presented a bleak vision of the future as a vacant inferno of sterilized sensation-seeking and the pointless pursuit of pleasure.

In 1937, Huxley discovered California, where he settled for most of the remainder of his life. There he developed an interest in mysticism and Eastern religions, and experimented with hallucinogenic substances such as peyote and mescalin.

At the time of his death, this American phase of his life seemed an uninteresting footnote to a once famous novelist's career. But the explosion of interest in consciousness-changing drugs and all forms of mysticism in the 'alternative culture' of the later 1960s was to lead to the rediscovery of Huxley as a prophet of psychedelia. Such books as *The Doors of Perception* and *Heaven and Hell*, containing descriptions of his mescalin experiences, would be avidly consumed by the hippies of Haight Ashbury.

Thirty years ago the place to be for the latest sound in music was the Cavern Club in Liverpool. Within the small and cramped area such famous names as Cilla Black, Gerry and the Pacemakers, and the Beatles were to emerge. Less well remembered today are the Mersey Beats, seen performing in the club in 1963. *The Hulton-Deutsch Collection Ltd*

the fire, but the squalor it represented was for many a recent, not a distant, memory.

Such key words as 'ecology', 'conservation' and 'heritage' had no place in the thought of 1963. It was a world in love with new technology and modernization. Do-it-yourself programmes on television explained how to rip out Victorian features from your home. The First Lady of the United States wore a real leopard-skin coat. Planners dreamed of glittering high-rise cities threaded by urban motorways. The Authorised Version of the Bible had been retranslated into English as functional as the new Swedish furniture. Even the Roman Catholic Church had just agreed that mass could be celebrated in the vernacular. The space age was six years old and a US President had promised to put a man on the Moon. The British and French governments had agreed to build a supersonic airliner and the United States was planning to follow suit. Xerox copying machines were beginning to transform office life, spelling the end of the typing pool. Transistors were making radios smaller and computers more compact and powerful.

There were plenty of perceived problems looming — overpopulation was much discussed, for example, and the possibility of nuclear war. But arguably more people viewed the future with at least a guarded optimism on 22 November 1963 than at any time since. Life had been getting wealthier, more comfortable, more fun for so long. Why should this ever end?

Hundreds of thousands of British teenagers woke on 22 November with a very special sense of anticipation and excitment. They were Beatles fans and this was the day scheduled for release of the Fab Four's new album, 'With The Beatles'. More than a quarter of a million fans had ordered copies of the LP in advance; most planned to collect the disc on Saturday morning and would drive their parents wild by playing the same tracks continuously

## BIRDMAN DIES

Alcatraz prison, where the famous Birdman, Robert Stroud, died on 22 November 1963. *The Hulton-Deutsch Collection Ltd*

On the morning of 22 November, the newspapers reported the death the previous day of Robert Stroud, known as the Birdman of Alcatraz, of 'natural causes and the infirmities of old age'.

Stroud had been imprisoned at the age of 20 for the manslaughter of a Russian bartender in the Alaskan goldfields. In prison, he murdered a particularly brutal guard. Sentenced to hang, he was reprieved eight days from his execution, but condemned to life imprisonment in solitary confinement.

Deprived of human contact, Stroud became interested in the birds that flew into the prison yard. He began to feed them, treat their ailments, and dissect them when they died. Over the years, he developed into a world authority on bird diseases and published books on the subject that were widely acclaimed.

In 1942 Stroud was transferred to the island prison of Alcatraz, off San Francisco. His bizarre life story made him a celebrity and he was portrayed by Burt Lancaster in a feature-length Hollywood biopic (*The Birdman of Alcatraz*, directed by John Falkenheimer, 1962). Despite campaigns for his release, however, fame did not bring any diminution of his sentence. When he died in hospital at Springfield, Missouri, at the age of 73, he was still a prisoner. He had spent almost 54 years in captivity, 43 of them in solitary confinement.

The clean cut, suit and tie image of the Beatles in the early 1960s; it would not be long before the psychedelic era of the hippy years made such an image appear old fashioned: *Lucy in the Sky with Diamonds* supplanting *Please, Please Me*. *The Hulton-Deutsch Collection Ltd*

**The Beatles in concert at the Grosvenor House Hotel barely a fortnight after Kennedy's assassination.** ***The Hulton-Deutsch Collection Ltd***

through the weekend — swooning as Paul sang 'All My Loving', gyrating in front of their mirror to 'Roll Over Beethoven' — probably near oblivious of dramatic events in the United States.

The edition of *New Musical Express* that came out on 22 November (trumpeting itself as having the 'world's largest circulation of any music paper — weekly sales exceed 250,000') pictured EMI chairman Sir Joseph Lockwood presenting the grinning Beatles with two silver LPs to mark sales of over a quarter of a million copies of each of their first two albums — 'Please Please Me', released the previous March, and 'With The Beatles'. George Martin, their recording manager, also presented each of the boys with a miniature silver EP for 'Twist and Shout', which had sold over 400,000 copies. The Beatles had already recorded a new single, 'I Want To Hold Your Hand' (flip side 'This Boy'), which would be released the following week. Advance sales had topped half a million, and it would be a golden disc within three days of arriving in the shops. The country was deluged in Beatles wigs, Beatles brooches, Beatles sweaters, Beatles collarless corduroy jackets, Beatles badges, Beatles books and magazines, Beatles pin-up photos, Beatles cartoons and even Beatles cakes. The record industry was already gearing up for a Beatles Christmas. Comedienne Dora Bryan's 'All I Want for Christmas Is a Beatle' was being heavily promoted after a successful airing on Juke Box Jury (the flip side was entitled 'If I Were a Fairy').

Despite their fame, on 22 November the Beatles were in the middle of another gruelling British tour, playing one-night stands throughout the provinces. They had reached the northeast and were performing that evening at the Stockton Globe.

Every edition of every newspaper had to have its Beatles feature. This does not seem as strange to us now as it did in 1963. That even the 'quality' newspapers were devoting space to a pop group was unprecedented. In the days leading up to 22 November there had been sensational saturation coverage of the Beatles' national tour — how they escaped a crowd of fans in Birmingham disguised as policemen, how hoses were turned on hysterical fans in Plymouth and so on.

The *TV Times* was running a series of weekly interviews with the boys, concentrating on one Beatle each issue. In a desperate bid to catch an appropriately zany tone, the magazine had entitled its series 'Reada Beatla Week'. The attempts to capture Beatle humour were also desperate. Here are Paul and Ringo discussing John:

Paul: And finally, of course, he went to the Royal College of Art.

Ringo: I don't remember that bit.

Paul: No, he didn't stay long.

Ringo: Why not?

Paul: Art didn't like him.

John informed the interviewer that the worst thing about the Beatles' fame was the mad scramble to get in and out of theatres alive, made more difficult for him personally because he was half-blind without his glasses: 'I've tried putting them on for our run-ins. But I hate them — and invariably they get knocked off anyway' (reminding us, incidentally, that this was before the days of contact lenses, even for the rich and famous).

On 22 November itself, the *Daily Express* offered its readers a track by track analysis of 'With The Beatles', concluding 'The fans will play it till it's transparent'. The *Daily Mirror* featured an article headlined 'Beatle Uniform for Schoolgirls', about sartorial changes at Ruffwood Comprehensive School at Kirkby near Liverpool:

'Gym slips and ankle socks are OUT for teenaged girls at one of Britain's biggest co-educational schools. Instead, the girls are to wear Beatle-style uniforms. The jacket — which the girls designed themselves — is right in the Beatles' groove. It has a round neck, with no lapels. With the jacket, the girls will wear candy-striped blouses, pleated skirts, nylons and chisel-toe shoes. And the whole uniform has the blessing of their headmaster.'

This story represented a progressive exception to the rule. Across the country, new youth styles were bringing teenagers into direct conflict with school authorities and, to a lesser extent, employers. Those two age-war battlefields of the sixties, short skirts and long hair, were not yet equally present. Fashionable skirts were still largely acceptable, but Beatle haircuts were not. It is hard, in retrospect, to see the Beatles of 1963 as having long hair at all, the famous cut looks neat and tidy to our eyes that have witnessed the excesses of Afros and Mohicans, yet it was universally perceived as long at the time. To the authorities, long hair signalled effeminacy and subversion. Boys who imitated their pop heroes were threatened with expulsion from school if they refused to 'get a haircut'. This, it appeared, was a line that must be held if order and civilisation were to be preserved. Thus style and revolt were inextricably linked. To be young and stylish in the sixties would involve a collision with authority, whether you wanted it to or not. Style made mild rebels of even the least rebellious youth.

The revolution in pop music and fashion was being led by young people a few years out of school — the generation born in the war years. Before 1963, the music industry had regarded pop singers as no more than faces and voices — pretty, clean-but-sexy boys and girls whose job it was to sell the songs churned out by the industry's hack tune-spinners. The British music business imitated American models slavishly. In a spirit of total cynicism, pop was manufactured by the old for consumption by the young. But the new groups were different. Their music had its own authenticity; it was produced by the young for the young. The impetus for the fresh sounds and styles came from below. Big business could still cash in on youth taste, but neither create nor control it.

The new wave of pop grew out of youth scenes at clubs and art colleges scattered across the country, where groups hammered out their own original versions of American rock 'n' roll and rhythm and blues. One of the most lively of these local scenes, in Liverpool, had briefly become the Mecca of pop in 1963. Record companies in search of the Liverpool sound signed up every local group they could find. The

**A star of an earlier generation, Marlene Dietrich meets The Beatles at the Royal Command Variety Performance on 4 November 1963. The concert, held at the Prince of Wales Theatre, was watched by Queen Elizabeth, the Queen Mother.**
***The Hulton-Deutsch Collection Ltd***

outbreak of Beatlemania had tended to overshadow the excitement surrounding the other beat groups that had sprung to prominence from the Mersey. Yet, earlier in the year the Beatles had not even held first place among the Liverpool bands breaking out into the national scene. Both the Searchers and Gerry and the Pacemakers (Gerry Marsden, his brother Freddie, Les Maguire and Les Chadwick) outsold the Beatles until the autumn.

The *NME* Top Thirty on 22 November showed the extraordinary dominance of the Mersey sound, with Liverpool groups occupying four of the top five places. The Beatles' 'She Loves You' had just pushed Gerry and the Pacemakers' 'You'll Never Walk Alone' down from number 1 to number 2. Another Liverpool group, Billy J. Kramer and the Dakotas, were at number 4 with the Lennon and McCartney number 'I'll Keep You Satisfied'. 'Sugar and Spice' from the Searchers was at 5. Although not from Liverpool, Freddie and the Dreamers at 7 with 'You Were Made For Me' and Brian Poole and the Tremeloes at 17 with 'Do You Love Me' shared in the same beat group fever. Mersey domination of the album chart was even more pronounced. The top three were the Beatles' 'Please Please Me' at 1, Gerry and the Pacemakers' 'How Do You Like It' at 2, and 'Meet The Searchers' at 3, while Freddie and the Dreamers were at 4.

Media coverage of the Liverpool groups was full of discomfort and ambivalence, disguised under a would-be humorous tone. They were seen as representing youth, the working class, and a potential for rebellion and irreverence that linked them vaguely to the spirit of the satire boom. The occasional encounters between these Liverpool street youths and royalty were a top focus of interest, as the Beatles Royal Command Performance had shown. There was clearly felt to be something unnatural and titillating about it, which had not been the case with other popular entertainers. It was perhaps that such events dramatised the sense of latent class conflict — working class youth getting above themselves — and at the same time resolved

***Right:*** **Three of the great names of Mersey music — Gerry Marsden (of Gerry and the Pacemakers), Cilla Black and Billy J. Kramer — all received silver discs in early 1964. One thing all three had in common, apart from their Mersey links, was that they were managed by Brian Epstein. *The Hulton-Deutsch Collection Ltd***

***Below:*** **The guru of the Mersey sound — Brian Epstein — with one of his protegés, Gerry Marsden. *The Hulton-Deutsch Collection Ltd***

it into a benign mist of classlessness.

At a London charity ball at the Savoy, *NME* reported on 22 November, Gerry and the Pacemakers 'had well and truly established the Merseyside sound with the mink and diamonds set'. Present were Princess Margaret and Lord Snowdon — and Gerry's mother, Mrs Marsden, prominently featured in the NME coverage. 'After seeing her sons Gerry and Fred playing for the Princess, she said: "It's the proudest moment of my life." The charity was in aid of the poor in Docklands, then still London's port area but in terminal decline. Gerry was allowed one of the cheeky remarks expected of Liverpudlians on such occasions: looking round the audience dripping with jewellery, he commented that 'dockers don't dress like this when they're on the dole.' But the rich onlookers were soon singing along to 'I Like It', even Princess Margaret 'clearly mouthing the words'. Gerry and his manager Brian Epstein were presented to the royal couple after the ball, which ended with the Temperance Seven (a novelty band

*Right:* **Three of the fresh faces of the early 1960s were given Variety Club awards in 1962 as most promising newcomers. Left to right we see Helen Shapiro, Cliff Richard and Rita Tushingham.** ***The Hulton-Deutsch Collection Ltd***

*Below:* **Headed by the drummer Dave Clark (seen front right), the Dave Clark Five was one UK group seeking to break the Liverpudlian monopoly of popular music. Pictured here on a trip to Los Angeles, they probably found North America a great deal more exciting than their native Tottenham.** ***The Hulton-Deutsch Collection Ltd***

well past their peak) playing the theme tune from the latest James Bond movie, *From Russia With Love*.

The triumphal advent of the Liverpool groups had shaken a whole range of performers and musical styles that had predominated in the early sixties. Cliff Richard was holding on against the new wave, still at number 3 on 22 November with 'Don't Talk To Him', and soon to be voted leading British male vocalist for the third year running. Adam Faith was struggling in the lower reaches of the singles chart and would soon abandon his singing career. Frank Ifield, who had topped the bill on the night the Beatles made their off-Mersey debut the previous year — and had been received with rapture while the Liverpool group fell flat — would never make a UK hit again. Helen Shapiro was on the way out. Acker Bilk and Kenny Ball were struggling in vain to keep some life in the tail-end of the traditional jazz craze. Singers like Frank Sinatra, Sammy Davis Jr and Andy Williams, who still featured prominently in the pop press at this time, would soon be

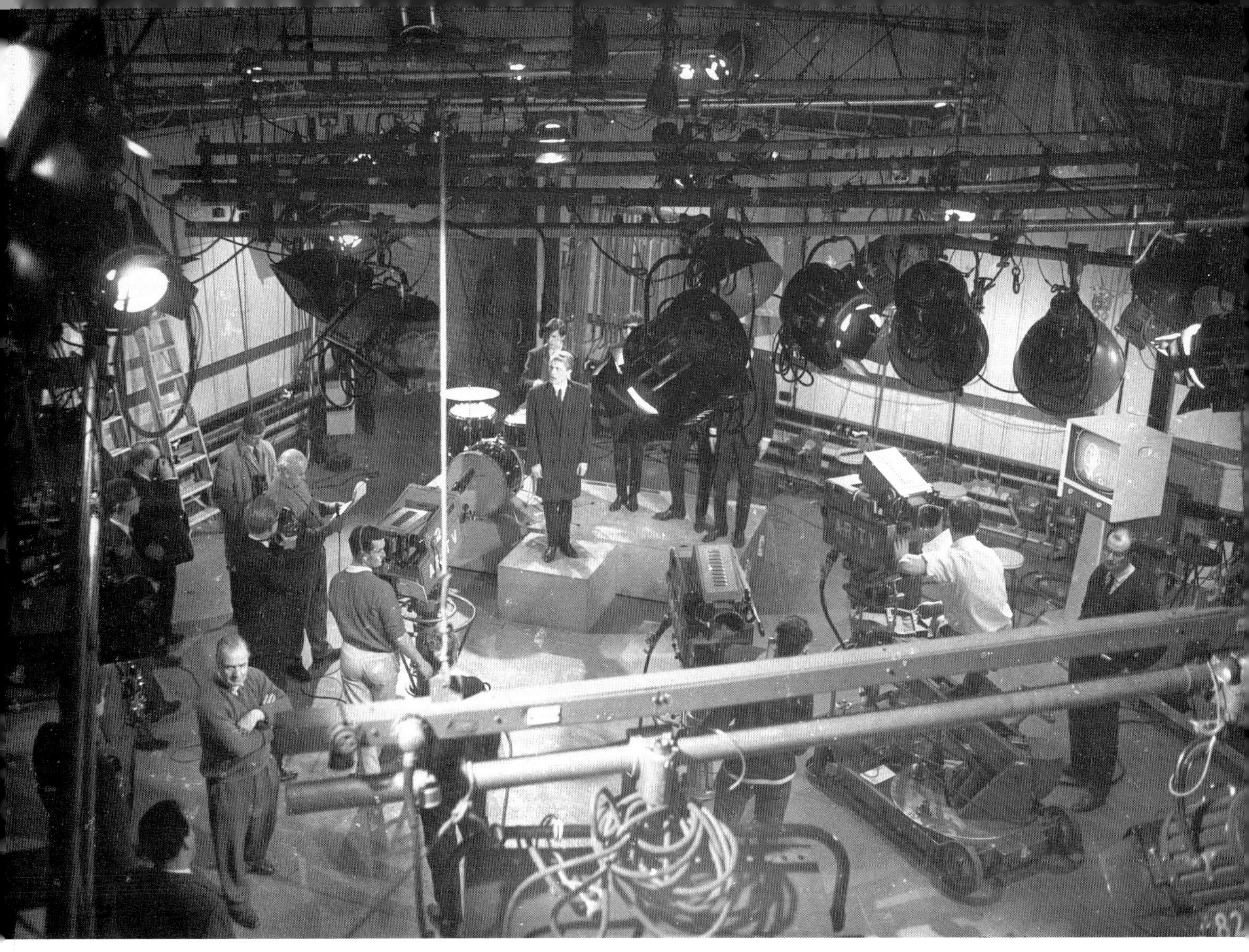

viewed as a quite different category of entertainer, irrelevant to the vital pop scene.

On the way up were the Dave Clark Five, who had just released 'Glad All Over', which would take them to the top. And the Rolling Stones were enjoying their first real success, with 'I Wanna Be Your Man' at number 23 in the singles chart. The Stones were being heavily promoted. On 22 November, they were booked to appear on *Ready, Steady, Go!*, and they had another television appearance the following night on *Thank Your Lucky Stars*. The *NME* announced that the Ronnettes would be touring in 1964 with the Rolling Stones among other British acts on the bill.

Despite the introduction of new programmes such as *Ready, Steady, Go!*, television coverage of pop was still lagging far behind the fans' level of interest. There was considerable excitement when the BBC announced they would record a half hour Beatles concert at the Liverpool Empire on 7 December for transmission the same evening. This was a most uncommon degree of coverage.

The one-night stand tour remained essential at a time when television performances were relatively rare and of poor quality, and before the invention of the pop video. On Friday, 22 November, the Beatles, Jaywalkers, Brook Brothers, and Vernon Girls were playing the Stockton Globe; Helen Shapiro, Bobby Rydell, and the Spotniks were at Sheffield City Hall; Billy J. Kramer and the Dakotas, Johnny Kidd, and the Caravelles were at Southampton Gaumont; Billy Fury, Joe Brown, Karl Denver, and the Tornados at Derby Gaumont; and Duane Eddy, the Shirelles, and Gene Vincent at Lewisham Gaumont.

The huge cinemas, the Gaumonts and Odeons that had been built in every town across the country during the film boom years and were now struggling to fill seats, offered the main venue for touring groups, along with municipal halls. Even for a group with a current hit in the top ten, the tour took in obscure provincial backwaters and locations lacking any pretentions to glamour. Brian Poole and the Tremeloes, for example, in December 1963 were to play at: Scampton RAF; Frome Grand

**The most popular of all music shows in 1963 was *Ready, Steady, Go!* introduced by Cathy McGowan. Seen amongst the clutter of the contemporary - black & white - television studio of the show is Adam Faith rehearsing for his appearance on the programme. Performers were constrained in their movements by the rudimentary television technology of the day. *The Hulton-Deutsch Collection Ltd***

Cinema; Swansea Tower; Llanelli Ritz; Coventry Matrix; Aldershot New Central; Manchester Princess and Domino; Isle of Man Villa Marina; Uxbridge Burtons; Liverpool Locarno; Nelson Imperial; Ilford Room at the Top; and Margate Dreamland. Tickets were around 6s or 7s (30p to 35p).

Touring was hard work and could be exhausting. A series of one-night stands in far from ideal buildings, with crummy dressing rooms often besieged by fans, microphones that never worked properly, sound systems too weak to be heard over the screams of the audience and hotels that were snooty about entertainers they regarded as yobs. Freddie Garrity of Freddie and the Dreamers informed the *NME* on 22 November that he would soon withdraw from touring to devote time to songwriting. He was suitably amusing on the unexpected hardships of life on the road:

'We have a nifty arrangement so that I can have a clean shirt as often as I can. I've got about 30 these days, and I kind of use a certain town or city as a base for clean laundry. If we're appearing in the Brighton area, for instance, I'll have a pile of clean shirts stored in London.'

**Exactly one month before Kennedy's death — on 22 October 1963 — Dusty Springfield was in the studio recording her latest song, *'I Only Want To Be With You'*. *The Hulton-Deutsch Collection Ltd***

This was before the age of the universal laundrette.

Freddie looked backed to 'the great times we used to have at the Cavern', and forward to fulfilling his ambition — to buy a big house outside Manchester. 'It'll take a bit of saving up, but I think it's a better investment than a posh car.' And sure enough, he wanted to move into cabaret — 'we could do a more polished act that way' — or films — 'I wouldn't mind a comedy film or something based on the group.'

This mixture of modest material ambitions and a desire to escape the dead-end of pop music for the world of 'all-round entertainment' characterized most pop singers of the time. An *NME* interview with the Shirelles, an American all-female group from New Jersey who had influenced the Beatles, revealed similar attitudes. There was the usual view of pop singing as merely a springboard to a proper career elsewhere. 'We'd like to develop into nightclub entertainers and move away from the rock 'n' roll field a little. This would give us a chance to become more sophisticated.' And they would like to be in films: 'A comedy would be nice.' The interview also revealed a timorous unfamiliarity with flying, still a mode of transport the majority of people had never experienced. 'Airplanes scare us. But we usually just buckle down the seat belt and pray!'

*NME*'s other interview of 22 November was with Dusty Springfield. The break-up of the Springfields was fresh news. Mary O'Brien, under her stage name of Dusty Springfield, already had a solo hit with 'I Only Want To Be With You', little over a month after splitting from the trio. *NME*'s Derek Johnson enthused about the boldness of Dusty's solo move:

'A challenging, tension-packed time for Dusty... an exciting, and perhaps memorable, time for the public, who may be about to witness the birth of a brilliant new star.'

With charming naïvety, Johnson informed his young readers that Dusty 'has a commercial outlook, which is so essential in these competitive days.' Interviewed over lunch, Dusty confided her ambition to become 'another Petula Clark'. She was booked to appear on television's *Thank Your Lucky Stars*. Johnson was struck by her ambition — and her taste in cars:

'As Dusty climbed into her new and very expensive Continental car, she called over her shoulder: "You know, I've just got to be a success to own a car like this!" Don't worry, Dusty — I'm sure you won't have to trade it in for a Mini.'

A significant sign of the times was the lack of US performers among the UK top sellers in November 1963. The top US entry in the *NME* 30 was the Ronnettes at 8 with the Phil Spector-produced 'Be My Baby'. Roy Orbison's 'Blue Bayou' and Shirley Bassey's 'I' were at 9 and 10. Lower down the chart were Rick Nelson with 'Fools Rush In', Trini Lopez's version of 'If I Had a Hammer' and Ray Charles singing 'Busted'. Peter, Paul and Mary singing Bob Dylan's 'Blowin' in the Wind' represented folk-protest at 13. Chuck Berry's 'Memphis Tennessee' was at 12 — a revival in interest in this 50s star growing as his influence on the Beatles and the Rolling Stones became public knowledge.

Turning to the US Top 20 singles published in *NME* on the same day, it is impossible to avoid an impression of comparative poverty of talent. Who remembers Dale and Grace (at number 1) or Jimmy Gilmer and the Fireballs, or the Village Stompers? A few legendary names leap to the eye: Elvis Presley with 'Bossa Nova Baby', the Beach Boys with 'Be True to Your School', Sam Cooke performing 'Little Red Rooster'and Roy Orbison with 'Mean Woman Blues'. But the future belonged to the British groups that were revitalising popular music — even transforming it into a phenomenon of a quite different scale and influence from anything that had been seen before. Soon there would be no more talk of becoming an all-round entertainer and no modest ambitions to own a posh car or a big house. Soon pop stars would be the kings of the world and their fortunes immense. But, on 22 November 1963, it was not quite yet.

The Beatles had so far failed to hit the charts in the United States, but they were beginning to attract American media attention. Filmed reports on Beatlemania appeared on all three US national TV networks in the week before the Kennedy assassination, the last of them on Thursday night, 21 November. As *NME* reported, US film crews had shot footage of the crowd hysteria during the Beatles' appearance at the Bournemouth Winter Gardens on the previous Saturday, 16 November. What most struck the Americans was the sensationally 'un-British' character of the fans behaviour. CBS interviewer Josh Darsa commented: 'I never thought a British audience could or would react this way for anyone — they certainly never went this wild for Johnnie Ray.' The fans took a nationalistic pride in flaunting their enthusiasm for the foreign cameras. According to *NME:* 'One teenage girl, sporting a Beatle haircut, Beatle sweater, and numerous Beatle pictures, declared: "We're showing the Yankees how we love our stars. Elvis never had it this good."' Darsa's presentation of the phenomenon to his own TV audience was patronizingly mocking and supercilious: he summed up the Beatles as 'non-musicians with non-haircuts'. This was an attitude that would not last the course. The Beatles were signed up for three appearances on the *Ed Sullivan Show* the following February. America didn't know what was about to hit it.

The remarkable rise of British pop culture was a revolt against the blank dreariness of the life that confronted young people on that smug little island. In the United States, at least for white youth, frustrations were less intense. Compared with Britain, the much-maligned American suburbs, with their neon dazzle and drive-in cinemas,

## WITH THE BEATLES

Released on 22 November 1963, the Beatles' second album marked a distinct shift in the group's image and pretentions. The cover was artistically posed and lit, grainy moody portraits of four intelligent young men in polo-necks — a world away from the simple cheery lads-next-door pictured on their first album, 'Please Please Me'. It looked like a modern jazz LP, implying serious creativity rather than the throw-away quality of pop.

The musical contents were still mainstream early Beatles, however — inventive numbers with a fresh, naïve sound, sometimes hard-driven, sometimes sentimental. The 14 tracks were: 'It Won't Be Long', 'All I've Got To Do', 'All My Loving', 'Don't Bother Me', 'Little Child', 'Till There Was You', 'Please Mister Postman', 'Roll Over Beethoven', 'Hold Me Tight', 'You Really Got A Hold On Me', 'I Wanna Be Your Man', 'Devil In Her Heart', 'Not A Second Time' and 'Money'. The album was exceptional in containing only previously unrecorded songs.

*Left:* **Beatlemania at its height: the 'Fab Four' playing in front of 15 million television viewers on *Sunday Night at the London Palladium. The Hulton-Deutsch Collection Ltd***

*Below left:* **A Beatles-crazed fan relaxes on the beach with reminders of the group. The group's fame had spread far and wide — as this Dutch admirer illustrates. The Beatles' first tour to the Netherlands started on 6 June 1964. *The Hulton-Deutsch Collection Ltd***

*Below:* **Social acceptability for the Beatles came with their appearance at the Royal Variety Performance on 6 November 1963. Also appearing were Harry H. Corbett and Wilfred Brambell (of television's *Steptoe and Son*), Tommy Steele, Harry Secombe, Max Bygraves, Eric Sykes, Hattie Jacques, Michael Flanders (in the wheelchair) and Donald Swann. *The Hulton-Deutsch Collection Ltd***

were a paradise for youth. The surfing beach parties to which suntanned Californian youths drove in their souped-up second-hand Chevys happened in a different universe. In Britain it was raining on the beach and the only way a young person could drive a fast car was to steal one.

The Beach Boys were the prime celebrants of the Californian lifestyle. They had initiated the surf rock boom with 'Surfin' Safari', 'Surfin' USA' and 'Surfer Girl', inspiring a whole school of imitators, such as the hunky sun-bleached duo Jan and Dean, whose 'Surf City' was an essential element of the soundtrack to summer 1963. By November, however, the Beach Boys — only one of whom could actually surf — had moved on to create a new craze: hot-rod music. Their album of automobile songs, 'Little Deuce Coupé', was a fixture in the charts through the autumn, with tracks such as '409', 'Our Custom Machine', and 'Cherry Cherry Coupé'.

The heroes of the American music scene often seemed to be the studios rather than the performers. Berry Gordy's Motown Corporation was flooding the market with hits from its stable of singers, including Mary Wells, Martha and the Vandellas, Marvin Gaye and 13-year-old little Stevie Wonder, who had topped both US singles and album charts in August. Philles Records, run by the innovative 22-year-old record producer

## Hot-rod songsters

The hot-rodding celebrated by the Beach Boys in 1963 was not, as it had been in the 1950s, the cult of home-made cars, with a high-power engine under the apparently innocent hood of an old banger. The 1960s hot-rods were factory-produced models deliberately targeted at the market for power and speed on the street.

The '409' hymned by the Beach Boys in the top hot-rod song of the year was the 1962 Chevrolet 409 Impala — the number referred to the cubic capacity of its V8 engine. Other hot-rod automobiles celebrated in song at around this time included the Pontiac GTO (Ronnie and the Daytonas, 'GTO') and the AC Cobra (the Rip Chords, 'Hey Little Cobra').

Phil Spector, had a series of successes with numbers sung by his girl groups the Crystals and the Ronettes ('Be My Baby', for example, and 'Then He Kissed Me'). Although Spector's 'wall of sound' recording technique, with its layering of blocks of instruments to create 'little symphonies for the kids', was an original and important step forward in pop music, however, it did not link into the emerging youth culture and contemporary political concerns with the same attention-grabbing potency as the other major innovation on the American popular music scene: the folk-protest boom.

Folk was the soundtrack of the political protest movement then sweeping the American student population; the songs of Bob Dylan, Joan Baez, Pete Seeger, Tom Paxton, Phil Ochs and others seemed to articulate the students' courage and despair, their fear of nuclear war, their desire for a peaceful world, their aspiration to equality and their hatred of injustice. At its worst, folk-protest was naïve and embarrassingly sentimental, feeding the American public's craving for the emotional gratification offered by liberal self-righteousness. At its best, especially in Dylan's finest songs — dense, obscure, harsh and monotonous, like no other popular music ever written — it had a raw power that was inspirational. One pop music writer who was a student in the early 1960s wrote: 'There was nothing more moving in the world of the Cuban

# Beatlemania

As a recognised phenomenon of British life, acknowledged daily by the national media and watched with fascination from abroad, analysed by psychologists and decried by politicians, denounced from some pulpits and welcomed from others, Beatlemania began on 13 October 1963.

The group's nationwide following had been growing throughout the year. It had been difficult at first to translate the adulation they enjoyed in Liverpool to a wider scene. Their first national tour in February 1963, when they were second on the bill to Helen Shapiro, caused no special scenes of frenzy. It was only after their hit singles 'Please Please Me' and 'From Me To You' that the breakthrough began. In May, when they toured with American singer Roy Orbison (whose extraordinary immobility and impassivity was a startling contrast to the moptops' jiggling wisecracking cheeriness), the first small riots broke out. Tickets were traded for large sums and items thrown at

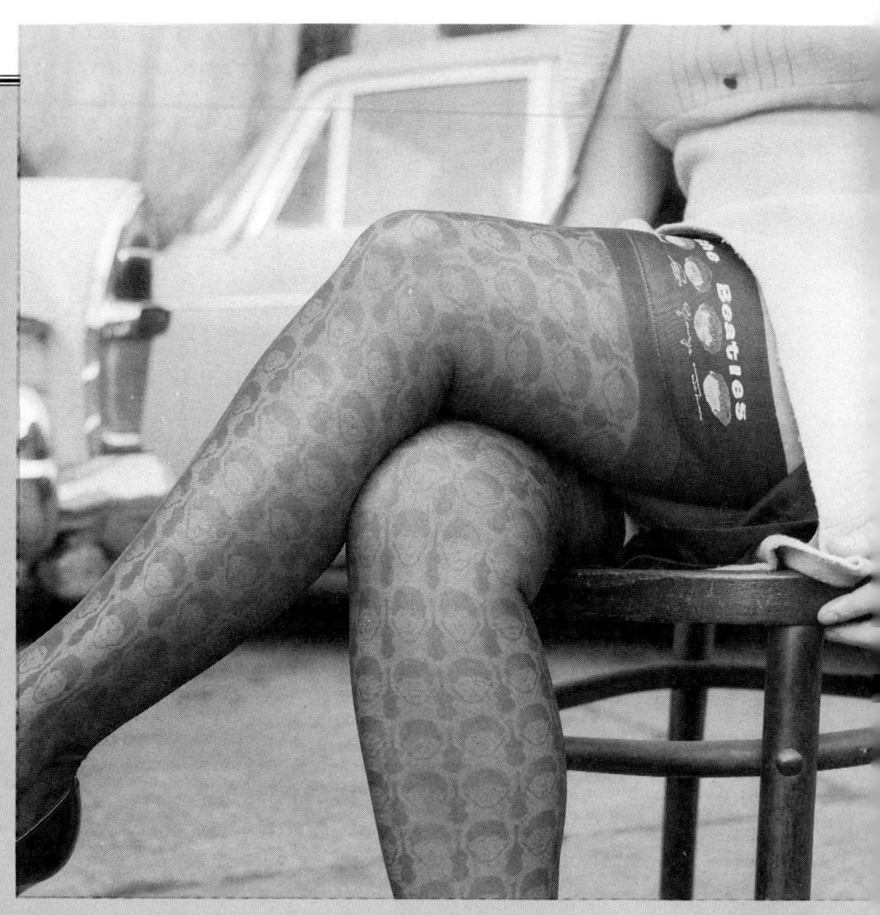

***Left:*** **Even fashion took account of the craze for the Beatles — stockings with the pictures of the four with their signatures being but part of what was a growth industry. *The Hulton-Deutsch Collection Ltd***

***Below left:*** **The Beatles' zany sense of humour was a refreshing change after the carefully groomed good manners of their immediate predecessors such as Cliff Richards and Adam Faith. *The Hulton-Deutsch Collection Ltd***

***Right:*** **The *Go! Go! Go!* column of the *Daily Express* on Friday 22 November previews the new Beatles' album, 'With The Beatles', giving a track-by-track critique of all the songs concluding 'The fans will play it till it's transparent'. Apart from the new LP, the Beatles were also at Number One in the Top 30 with *She Loves You*. Also doing well were Gerry and the Pacemakers, Cliff Richard and, with a new entry at Number 17, Dusty Springfield.**

## Arrow 'Apaches' attack wagon trains

Express Staff Reporter

A GANG of "Apaches" is terrorising train and van drivers with deadly steel arrows.

One of the arrows, with blazing, petrol-soaked rag fastened to the end, embedded itself in the side of a goods wagon.

The woodwork was scorched.

Another of the two-feet-long arrows pierced the side of a Lyons bread van. A second van was also hit.

All the incidents have happened at Brislington, Somerset, near the main Bristol - London railway line.

*ON TARGET*

Mr. Stanley Butt, sales manager of the Lyons bread depot at Brislington, said last night: "These idiots are using the 'O' in our name as a moving target. One shot was almost dead centre."

A British Railways police official said: "This is a bit of Apache warfare gone crazy. These arrows could easily kill. Train drivers have been warned to keep a sharp look-out."

The arrows are made of metal with steel heads welded to the end. They are fletched with stiff cardboard.

## Queen's message to blood donors

One million blood donors yesterday received through the post a message from the Queen praising their services.

The message, in a leaflet entitled "Life Blood," said their example should inspire yet more to join them.

## GO! GO! GO!

# Track by track—new Beatles LP

MORE THAN 400,000 SOLD ALREADY

BY JANE GASKELL

**TOP 30**

(Last week's placing in brackets.)

| |  |  | |
|---|---|---|---|
| 1 | SHE LOVES YOU | Beatles | (2) |
| 2 | YOU'LL NEVER WALK ALONE | Gerry and the Pacemakers | (1) |
| 3 | DON'T TALK TO HIM | Cliff Richard | (5) |
| 4 | I'LL KEEP YOU SATISFIED | Billy J. Kramer | (8) |
| 5 | SUGAR AND SPICE | Searchers | (3) |
| 6 | SECRET LOVE | Kathy Kirby | (6) |
| 7 | YOU WERE MADE FOR ME | Freddie and the Dreamers | (13) |
| 8 | BE MY BABY | Ronettes | (4) |
| 9 | MARIA ELENA | Los Indios Tabajaras | (12) |
| 10 | BLUE BAYOU | Roy Orbison | (9) |
| 10 | I | Shirley Bassey | (7) |
| 12 | MEMPHIS TENNESSEE | Chuck Berry | (10) |
| 13 | IT'S ALMOST TOMORROW | Mark Wynter | (19) |
| 14 | BLOWIN' IN THE WIND | Peter, Paul, and Mary | (16) |
| 15 | FOOLS RUSH IN | Rick Nelson | (14) |
| 16 | THEN HE KISSED ME | Crystals | (15) |
| 17 | DO YOU LOVE ME | Brian Poole and the Tremeloes | (11) |
| 17 | I ONLY WANT TO BE WITH YOU | Dusty Springfield | (—) |
| 19 | IF I HAD A HAMMER | Trini Lopez | (17) |
| 20 | MONEY | Bern Elliott and the Fenmen | (—) |
| 20 | YOUR MOMMA'S OUT OF TOWN | Carter-Lewis | (24) |
| 20 | DEEP PURPLE | Nino Tempo and April Stevens | (—) |
| 23 | I WANNA BE YOUR MAN | Rolling Stones | (21) |
| 24 | BEATLES VOL. 1 (EP) | Beatles | (27) |
| 25 | MISS YOU | Jimmy Young | (28) |
| 26 | BUSTED | Ray Charles | (20) |
| 27 | GLAD ALL OVER | Dave Clark Five | (—) |
| 27 | THE FIRST TIME | Adam Faith | (17) |
| 29 | TWIST AND SHOUT (EP) | Beatles | (—) |
| 30 | BEATLES HITS (EP) | Beatles | (—) |

By arrangement with New Musical Express.

OUT TODAY, with over 400,000 advance sales, the new Beatles LP **WITH THE BEATLES** (Parlophone PMC 1206) is going to be one huge smash hit whether or not it deserves to be.

The initial Beatles LP **Please Please Me**, out last May, sold altogether nearly as much as **pre-release** sales of this one. Recording company E.M.I. claims this colossal advance order has never before been equalled in Britain.

Teenagers galore have ordered **WITH THE BEATLES** without even hearing it. How excited will they be when they settle back to listen?

### Distinction

Track one—**IT WON'T BE LONG**, written by Lennon and McCartney—is one of the gladdest "You're Comin' Home" songs. There's expectation of ecstatic reunion in every line Lennon punches out.

**ALL I'VE GOT TO DO**: John, with Paul harmonising behind him, takes this at a nice slow pace, a sort of emotional breather.

**ALL MY LOVING**: George's guitar solo gives a rollicky distinction to this rather bluesy chant.

**DON'T BOTHER ME**: This is George Harrison's debut as a composer. George's voice, two tracks combined, duets with himself a despairing sort of lyric—he's lost the only girl for him. Everyone else can push off. He's not interested.

On **LITTLE CHILD** Paul lays down his guitar and plays piano. John adds mouth-organ bars at another mike.

**TILL THERE WAS YOU**: Paul sings this straight, no gimmicks.

**PLEASE MISTER POSTMAN**: Because this track is repetitive and so hypnotic it grows on you.

Now turn over to side two. **ROLL OVER BEETHOVEN** is a fascinating track, the Merseyside accent in action doing weird things with the master's name.

### Exciting

**HOLD ME TIGHT**: Fine, fast, urgy number from Paul.

**YOU REALLY GOTTA HOLD ON ME**: The most exciting track of the entire LP. Lyrics give a powerful picture of the love that isn't right but is too precious to give up for a moment.

**I WANNA BE YOUR MAN**: An energetic demand from Ringo, with Hammond organ chords by courtesy of Lennon.

**DEVIL IN HER HEART**: Wistful medium-pace, better to dance to.

**NOT A SECOND TIME**: John sings with himself, a routine "It's Over" dirge.

**MONEY**: The words of this are pretty outright. The force builds up to a raw-throated, tension-taut climax guaranteed to send any audience half-crazy.

The Beatles have never previously recorded anything on this LP. The fans will play it till it's transparent.

EVERY WEEK IN THE EXPRESS

## Acker Bilk

WHERE have all the big bands gone? Twenty years ago there were more of them about than you could wave a baton at; today they are as rare as teetotal trombone players or shy, retiring drummers.

the stage, including jellybabies, became a minor hazard of performance. By September they had the top selling LP, 'Please Please Me', the best selling EP, 'Twist and Shout', and the best selling single, 'She Loves You' (which made 'Yeh, Yeh' a national catch phrase).

On 13 October the Beatles were the star attraction on British television's top variety show, *Sunday Night At The London Palladium*. The Palladium theatre in the West End was besieged by screaming, chanting fans throughout the day. When they left at the end of the performance, Paul, John, George and Ringo were almost torn apart in the 50-yard dash to their car. The London-based media, which had until then largely ignored the Beatles, suddenly awoke to a major news story. The crowd frenzy featured on the front pages, where it would stay for month after month.

Wherever the Beatles toured, fans queued all night for tickets. The screaming and shrieking of young girls during their concerts became a ritual — as Hunter Davies wrote, girls 'foamed at the mouth, burst into tears, hurled themselves like lemmings in the direction of the Beatles, or just simply fainted'. No one could actually hear the group's music live; the audience provided most of the noise and the drama. There was a riot when they visited Stockholm at the end of October, and extraordinary scenes when they flew back to London — the first of those mass airport welcomes that were to become so familiar over the following years.

On 4 November the Beatles played at the *Royal Command Performance* ('She Loves You', 'Till There Was You', and 'Twist and Shout') in front of the Queen Mother, Princess Margaret and her then husband Lord Snowdon. John Lennon made his joke: 'Will people in the cheaper seats clap your hands. The rest of you rattle your jewellery', and their lovability was confirmed for 26 million TV viewers.

There were a few negative reactions to Beatlemania. The *Daily Telegraph* grumbled that the mass hysteria was reminiscent of Nazi rallies. Paul Johnson, in the left-wing *New Statesman*, wrote snootily: 'Those who flock round the Beatles, who scream themselves into hysteria, whose vacant faces flicker over the TV screens, are the least fortunate of their generation, the dull, the idle, the failures.' But the more common response among older people was tolerant amusement. With their zany, irreverent interview style and their cheeky charm, they seemed the embodiment of youth and fun, two qualities the world was generally agreed to be in need of. A Liverpool housewife interviewed by the *Evening Standard* summed up the Beatles' comfortable appeal for non-teenagers: 'They look depraved,' she said, 'in the nicest possible way.'

Most observers in November 1963 would have supposed that the Beatles phenomenon had reached its peak and would soon fade. The next 12 months would show that it had hardly begun.

## Record prices

Being a pop fan was not cheap in November 1963. LPs were selling for around 30s 0d (£1.50), EPs for 12s 0d (60p), and singles for about 6s 8d (33p). In relation to current wage levels, LPs were at least as expensive as top price CDs are today (Foyles record shop was advertising in the *NME* for 'experienced staff' at £18 a week); there was even a flourishing market in selling albums on hire purchase, at 2s 6d a week. People's record collections were generally much smaller than is common now, each disc listened to more often and more fervently.

Most albums were released in mono and stereo versions . No teenager was likely to be able to afford stereo equipment, although their parents might have a radiogram, a solid piece of furniture with two built-in speakers. There were no cassettes, of course. Young people listened to their discs on small single-speaker record players, the most sophisticated feature of which was the automatic system for playing stacks of singles.

**For the music fan of the early 1960s mono recordings were still the norm and singles the accepted way of acquiring record collections. Most equipment was still simple, although more sophisticated stacking systems — such as this Bush player — were becoming more popular.** ***The Hulton-Deutsch Collection Ltd***

missile crisis and CND than to listen to Dylan singing "Masters of War" and "Hard Rain".'

Folk had broken through to mainstream commercial success during the summer of 1963, and on 22 November folk singers Peter, Paul and Mary were top of the US album charts for the fourth week running with 'In The Wind', which had taken over the spot from their previous album, the eponymous 'Peter, Paul and Mary'. 'In The Wind' was, of course, a reference to Bob Dylan's 'Blowin' in the Wind', which Peter, Paul and Mary had taken into the top singles charts during the summer, as they had another Dylan song, 'Don't Think Twice, It's All Right'.

Commercially and politically, Peter, Paul and Mary were the more acceptable face of folk-protest for Middle America. Other prominent performers and song writers, such as Pete Seeger, Joan Baez and Dylan were regarded with suspicion. The *Hootenanny* show on America's ABC-TV network, a programme which since its inception in April 1963 had done much to popularize the new folk music, refused to show singers suspected of left-wing views — which included almost all the top folk-protest performers. Pete Seeger was banned before the programme even got started, because he rejected ABC's demand that he swear an oath of loyalty to the United States. Joan Baez refused to appear on the programme because she was not allowed to sing politically hard-hitting songs. Dylan had his own problems with television, walking out of rehearsals for the *Ed Sullivan Show* in May because he was not allowed to sing 'Talkin' John Birch Society Blues', an explicit attack on American right-wing extremism.

Although Dylan's bleak and tuneless delivery had retarded his performing career, by November 1963 he was emerging as the unquestioned prince of the folk movement. After his first solo concert in April at Town Hall in New York City, *Billboard* magazine had described him as 'the stuff of which legends are made.' On 26 October he performed to a sell-out crowd at the prestigious Carnegie Hall in New York. 'The Freewheelin' Bob Dylan', his second album, including songs such as 'Girl From the North Country' and 'Masters of War', sold over a quarter of a million copies in the first six months after its release. With Joan Baez playing, as *Newsweek* put it, 'princess to his prince among young folk fans', Dylan was poised on the brink of superstardom. Whether he was already uncomfortable with his rôle as a messiah of political protest is not clear, but within a year he was largely to abandon both protest and folk.

## Spector's Christmas

Recently released on 22 November 1963 was record producer Phil Spector's Christmas compilation album, 'A Christmas Gift To You'. The album was designed as a showcase for Spector's 'wall of sound' recording style. Spector hoped to raise a set of pop Yuletide standards — 'Santa Claus is Coming to Town', 'Silent Night' — to symphonic status by the technical quality of the arrangements (by Jack Nitzche) and the sound. The performers were the top names from the Philles label: the Crystals, the Ronettes, Darlene Love and Bob B. Sox and the Blue Jeans.

When he heard of Kennedy's death, Spector immediately withdrew the album from the stores as a gesture of grief and respect, commenting that 'nobody's going to want happy Christmas songs this year.' As a result, 'A Christmas Gift For You' sank into oblivion, but it is now highly prized as the peak of Spector's achievement as a record producer.

As Kennedy was driving through the happy crowds on Main Street, Dallas, millions of British families were asking the key question of every evening: 'What's on the box?' Although the box was a black-and-white (or, more honestly, grey) screen, 19 inches or smaller, it exercised a fascination over the families that clustered around its flickering light far greater than today's 'satellite-linked colour-with-video-plus-teletext-deluxe-multichannel' models.

One reason was obviously novelty, the majority of people had owned or rented a television for six or seven years at most. In 1953 there had been just over two million TV licences issued in Britain; by 1958 the figure was over eight million, and by 1963 almost 12.5 million (the annual licence cost £4). People had only recently broken themselves of the habit of watching television in a darkened room, by analogy with cinema. They were seeing virtually the first generation of soap operas (*Coronation Street* was two years old), American TV adventure series, crime thrillers and medical dramas.

A less obvious reason for television's hold over the population of 1963 was the existence of only two channels, with no competition from videos. This made television watching far more of a participation in a communal experience — when you went to work the following day, almost everyone had seen the same popular programmes you had seen. Each favourite was more of a special occasion when

22

**TV and Radio for today**

STAR SPOT

BRENDA BRUCE is guest in "Dr. Finlay's Casebook" tonight, starring with Andrew Cruickshank and Barbara Mullen. B.B.C., 8.10.

**BBC-TV**

9.40-10.45 FOR SCHOOLS: 9.40-10.0 Pure Mathematics, Year II. 10.2-10.22 Middle School Mathematics. 10.25 Cymru A'I Phobl: For Welsh Schools.
10.45-11.0 WATCH WITH MOTHER.
11.5-11.55 FOR SCHOOLS: 11.5-11.25 Spotlight: People-Politics-Problems. 11.35-11.55 Indoors And Out.
1.0 NEWYDDION. 1.5 HEDDIW.
1.25 NEWS.
1.30-1.45 WATCH WITH MOTHER.
2.5-2.25 FOR SCHOOLS: The Orchestra.
5.10 TIME FOR TICH: Comedy, Puzzles.
5.35 HOBBIES CLUB. 6.0 NEWS.
6.10 TOWN AND AROUND. WEATHER.
6.35 LOOK: Fish Families.
7.0 POINTS OF VIEW. 7.5 TONIGHT.
7.45 HERE'S HARRY: The Musician, starring Harry Worth, with Max Jaffa, Edwin Apps, Geoffrey Hibbert, and Doris Gambell.
8.10 DR. FINLAY'S CASEBOOK: The Face Saver. Guest star, Brenda Bruce.
9.0 NEWS.
9.10 THE DICK VAN DYKE SHOW: The Sleeping Brother.
9.35 BRITTEN AT FIFTY: Profile of Benjamin Britten.
10.40 TOP IN TELEVISION: Dinner and ball of the Guild of Television Producers and Directors. The guild's awards for 1963.
11.10 NEWS EXTRA. 11.25 WEATHER.
11.27-11.57 LLIF BYWYD.

**ITV-LONDON**

2.35-3.41 FOR SCHOOLS: 2.35-3.0 Afternoon Edition. 3.4-3.22 Story Box: Nature, looking at Sea Anemones. 3.26-3.41 Notre Ville: Le Frère.
4.45 SMALL TIME: Muskit and Dido.
5.0 FIVE O'CLOCK CLUB. Guests Eileen Duffy and Dave Berry and the Cruisers.
5.25 QUICK DRAW MCGRAW.
5.55 NEWS. WEEKEND WEATHER.
6.15 READY, STEADY GO! The Weekend Starts Here.
7.0 TAKE YOUR PICK: starring Michael Miles.
7.30 EMERGENCY—WARD 10, with Desmond Carrington, Paula Byrne.
8.0 ROUTE 66. Man out of Time, starring Martin Milner and George Maharis.
8.55 NEWS.
9.10 FRIDAY NIGHT PRESENTS: Green Rub.
10.5 BOYD Q.C., starring Michael Denison with Charles Leno in By Gas—that's Murder.
10.35 NEWS HEADLINES.
10.37 ROVING REPORT.
11.2 DATELINE WESTMINSTER. WEATHER.
11.22 THE WINNERS: TV Awards 1963.
11.35 THE ADVENTURES OF THE SEA-HAWK: Search at Sea.
11.55 EPILOGUE: Peace, by the Rev. Kenneth Gibbons.

ITV REGIONS AS ITV LONDON EXCEPT AS SHOWN.

**ITV—Southern**

6.5 Day by Day. Southern News. 6.40-7.0 Out of Town. 8.0-8.55 The Greatest Show on Earth. 11.20 The Story of a Matador. 11.50 Weather. The Living Word.

**ITV—Channel**

4.40-4.45 Puffin's Birthday Greetings. 6.5 Channel News. Weather. 6.15 Patrick O'Hagen Sings. 6.30-7.0 Channel Newsweek. 10.5-10.35 Dial 999. 10.37 University Challenge. 11.5 Pony Express. 11.35 Dateline. 11.45 French News. Weather.

**ITV—Westward**

4.48 Westward News Headlines. 4.50-5.0 Playtime. 6.5 Westward News. Weather. 6.15 Westward Diary. 6.35 Westward Gazette. 6.45-7.0 Sports Report. 10.5-10.35 Dial 999. 10.37 University Challenge. 11.5 Pony Express. 11.35 Dateline. 11.50 The Winners: TV Awards 1963. 12.0 Weather. Faith for Life.

**ITV—Northern**

3.40-5.0 Close. 5.25-5.55 Supercar. 6.5 Mister Ed. 6.30-7.0 Scene at 6.30. 8.0-8.55 Bonanza. 10.35 Thirty-Minute Theatre: The Desperate Man on Platform 10. 11.5 News Headlines. Newscast. 11.20-11.55 Late Scene. Goodnight.

**ITV—W. and S.W.**

4.24 Newyddion y Dydd. 4.29-5.0 Tregampau. 5.25-5.55 Richard the Lionheart. 6.5 TWW Reports. 6.13 Movie Magazine. 6.42-7.0 Here Today. 8.0-8.55 Bonanza. 10.5 In the News. 10.35 The Alfred Hitchcock Hour. 11.35 The Summing Up. 11.40 Weather.

**ITV—Wales W. and N.**

Programme opens with 4.40-4.45 Birthday Club. 5.25-5.55 Supercar. 6.6 Here's Roger Price. 6.15 Tregampau. 6.45-7.0 Success Story. 8.0-8.55 Bonanza. 10.5-10.35 In the News. 11.3 Movie Magazine. 11.30-11.35 Profile. Close.

**ITV—Midland**

12.45 Thought for the Day. 12.47-1.22 Lunch Box, with News Flash at 1. 3.26-3.46 For Schools: Movement: The Flight of a Bird. 3.46-5.0 Close. 5.25-5.55 Supercar. 6.5-6.15 Midlands News. 8.0-8.55 Bonanza. 10.5 Police Five. 10.10 Film: Pickwick Papers. Weather. 11.55 Epilogue.

**ITV—Anglia**

5.25-5.55 The Junior Angle Club. 6.5 About Anglia. 6.45-7.0 Arena. 8.0-8.55 Bonanza. 10.5-10.35 Tavern Topics. 11.20 Anglia News Headlines. Weather. 11.24 Not for Hire. 11.50 Epilogue.

**WINNERS**

KEMPTON: Going good

**TODAY'S LISTENING**



**Riddle-Me-Ree**

**Today's fixtures**

The television page of the *Daily Express* for 22 November 1963 showing the day's entertainment. There were only two television channels, whilst BBC radio was divided into *Home* (effectively now Radio 4), *Light* (Radio 2) and the *Third* (Radio 3). It was to be another four years before a radio channel devoted to popular music was launched by the BBC; in the meantime the commmercial Radio Luxembourg had the teenage market to itself.

## YOUNG BOB

It was evident even in November 1963 that Bob Dylan did not really fit the simplistic image of an idealistic folk singer dedicated to political activism and good causes, although this was the image that captivated his early audiences. That month *Newsweek* ran a hostile article on the newly emerging star that sought to wise young people up to the true nature of their hero.

This is how *Newsweek* introduced Dylan to its readers:

'He popped up out of nowhere, another unknown, unscrubbed face in Greenwich Village, and now, only two years later, he sits in the pantheon of the folk-music movement. His name is Bob Dylan, he is 22 years old, and his bewildered brown-blond hair trails off into uneven sideburns. He sticks his skinny frame into blue jeans and wrinkled shirts, and he talks hip talk, punctuated with obscenities. His singing voice scratches and shouts so jarringly that his success, at first, seems incredible. Yet his knack for stirring audiences is unmistakable, and it stems, mainly, from the words of the some 200 songs he has written, simple words that pounce upon the obvious — the inequalities, dangers, and deceits of the 1960s — and hammer them home.

**One of the hottest musical talents to emerge from the United States at this time was Bob Dylan. His folk songs seemed to encapsulate the mood of protest and rebellion that was developing amongst a section of white American youth.**
***The Hulton-Deutsch Collection Ltd***

Newsweek was heavily sarcastic about the naivety of Dylan's admirers, mostly high school and college students, who worshipped the singer/songwriter because he seemed to have experienced the same angst that they felt themselves. The magazine parodied students talking hip about their hero: 'He has suffered; he has been hung up, man, without bread, without a chick, with twisted wires growing inside him.' This identification with the suffering folk singer was the secret of Dylan's appeal.

*Newsweek* was then at pains to inform its readers of Dylan's carefully concealed respectable background as Bobby Zimmerman of Hibbing, Minnesota, and of his keen interest in the financial rewards of recording contracts. It even alleged that 'Blowin' in the Wind' had not been written by Dylan at all, but by a student called Lorre Wyatt.

Dylan's anger at this attack was long-lasting. The *Newsweek* article confirmed his suspicious and defensive attitude toward the press that would last a lifetime. The magazine was partially right, however, in its critique of the flaws in Dylan's relationship with his politically motivated, purist folk audience. He would soon disillusion many of his early followers by abandoning the acoustic guitar, 'going electric', and withdrawing into the aloof pose of the superstar.

# Pop on telly

In November 1963, British television and radio were still struggling, often unsuccessfully, to adapt to the explosion of youth culture and music. There were three regular pop programmes on television: *Juke Box Jury*, introduced by David Jacobs, *Thank Your Lucky Stars* fronted by Brian Matthew and *Ready, Steady, Go!*

Both *Juke Box Jury* and *Thank Your Lucky Stars* were firmly under adult control, adopting a tolerant and patronising parental tone. The dullness of *Juke Box Jury*, the visuals consisted exclusively of Jacobs and four far-from-young celebrities fiddling with pens or nodding their heads while the records played, was only alleviated by the game-show format (voting hit or miss) and the interesting embarrassment when the 'jury' panned a record whose performer was secretly present behind a screen. There was also the chance of generating some interest by inviting performers to join the 'panel': the Beatles were to provide the four-man 'jury' on 7 December.

*Ready, Steady, Go!* was the only TV show to capture at least some of the excitement of pop in 1963. It had employed a 19-year-old secretary from Streatham, Cathy McGowan, as 'teenage adviser', and would soon use her to front the show. Described by the show's creator, Elkan Allan, as 'gauche and raw' but 'terribly switched on in a teenage way', McGowan became for a few years one of the most famous personalities in Britain.

What made *Ready, Steady, Go!* was not the performances, most acts mimed to their records, but the audience. When Gerry and the Pacemakers sang 'You'll Never Walk Alone' on the programme on 22 November (a performance broadcast just before news arrived of Kennedy's agony in Dallas), the hysterical, tear-stained expressions on the faces of girls in the audience established real contact with the extraordinary power of pop in 1963.

***Above:*** **A fortnight before Kennedy's death, on 9 November, Billy J. Kramer starred on ABC's *Thank Your Lucky Stars. The Hulton-Deutsch Collection Ltd***

***Left:*** **The rudimentary nature of pop music shows on television is emphasised by this shot of The Searchers on the 200th edition of *Lucky Stars.* No strobes or funny camera angles, just a display of various chocolate types. *The Hulton-Deutsch Collection Ltd***

## Before the Pirates

BBC radio, which still had a monopoly of broadcasting in the United Kingdom, made even less allowance for the sort of popular music the young were interested in than television did. There were only three services: the Home Service, the Light Programme and the Third Programme. The music on the Third Programme was classical, and on the Home Service light classical. That left the Light Programme, which was occupied to a large degree by non-musical broadcasting. On 22 November, its programming included the *Dales, Woman's Hour,* the *Archers,* the *Navy Lark,* the *Flying Doctor, Any Questions?,* and three programmes featuring BBC light orchestras. During the whole day, there was no space for pop music at all.

The *Billy Cotton Band Show* was still the major Light Programme vehicle for pop singers. No wonder young people tuned in to Radio Luxembourg, and flocked to listen to Radio Caroline and Radio Atlanta when pirate broadcasting began the following year.

there was so little choice. Hence the loyalty and devotion that fans felt for programmes such as *The Avengers*, *Dr Who*, or *Z Cars*, and the extraordinary dominance that a single variety show could exercise — in the United States, the *Ed Sullivan Show* on CBS, and in Britain, Val Parnell's *Sunday Night at the London Palladium* with its gimmick of the revolving stage, the Tiller Girls and Bruce Forsyth's mini-game show *Beat the Clock*. A third channel was on its way for British viewers. The *Radio Times* was advertising its new programming for BBC 2, to be launched in 1964. There was to be a whole evening a week devoted to higher education (this was later overtaken by the Open University concept) and 'the finest Continental film we can buy' on Sundays. It would be a long time before this upmarket experience was available to most people, however. Even if you lived in the right transmission area, you needed a new 625 line set, priced at around £70 — about a month's factory wages. BBC 2 was also eventually promising colour. Four million Americans already had colour TV, but the British would not begin to experience it in any great numbers until the end of the decade.

Technically most British productions were primitive. Although some comedy and drama was still broadcast live, most was now prerecorded in the studio on videotape, with film inserts for the occasional outside shot or more complex action sequence. There was little opportunity for camera movement in these low-budget studio-bound productions, so most scenes were as static as they would have been during the early days of talking cinema. Seeing again, for example, early episodes of *The Avengers* thirty years on, the technical woodenness of the presentation makes it almost impossible to become involved in the drama.

But television was attracting some of the best writers, the most inventive minds, and the most ambitious go-getters of that generation. And this gave many of British television's products a freshness that would be hard to match later. It could be

***Right:*** **Early evening viewing on BBC was dominated by 50 minutes of drama: *Dr Finlay's Casebook*. This popular series, based on the characters created by A. J. Cronin, portrayed life in a Scottish medical practice. It starred Barbara Mullen as the housekeeper Janet, Andrew Cruickshank as Dr Cameron and Bill Simpson as Dr Finlay. *The Hulton-Deutsch Collection Ltd***

*Left: The Dick Van Dyke Show* **— imported from the United States — followed the BBC's news at 9pm. Here the programme's eponymous star is seen with Irene Ryan on 14 October 1963 at a ball in Beverly Hills.** *The Hulton-Deutsch Collection Ltd*

remarkably easy for quite young people either to appear on television or have their material shown there, if they had the requisite pushiness. A remarkable number of the established television personalities of the 1980s and 1990s were already on screen in 1963 (for example, Bruce Forsyth, David Frost, Alan Whicker, George Cole, Cliff Michelmore, Robert Robinson).

So what were British viewers expecting to see on Friday, 22 November 1963? At 6.00 p.m. they were watching the news, because there were only two channels and the news was on both of them. Those who intended to devote their evening to the BBC could then look forward to learning about the fascinating courtship behaviour of the stickleback in Peter Scott's regular nature programme, *Look*, followed by Robert Robinson's sardonic presentation of viewers' letters in *Points of View*. *Tonight* was the centrepiece of BBC's weekday early evening schedule, covering serious events of the day and amusing trivia. The programme could field an impressive team, with Cliff Michelmore as main presenter, Alan Whicker, Derek Hart, Fyfe Robertson, Macdonald Hastings, Julian Pettifer and Brian Redhead.

Next in line was comedian Harry Worth in *Here's Harry*, to be supported that evening by a surprising comic appearance by suave violinist Max Jaffa. The heart-warming medical drama of *Dr Finlay's Casebook* led up to the *Nine O'Clock News*, followed by an imported American comedy, the *Dick Van Dyke Show* (in which Mary Tyler Moore and Dick van Dyke introduced the British public to the startling notion of separate beds for married couples). A serious note returned with a 65-minute celebration of Benjamin Britten's 50th birthday, introduced by the doyen of cultural television presenters, Huw Wheldon. Then David Coleman would front an outside broadcast of the British TV Awards ceremony for 1963, before the BBC's evening ended in Welsh with *Llif Bywyd*.

Commercial television in London began

## Telstar

In 1963 television was still far from linking the whole world in what Marshall McLuhan was to call 'the global village'. The first ever transatlantic broadcast was made via the communication satellite Telstar at 1 a.m. on 11 July 1962, showing the pre-recorded face of Frederick R. Kappel, the chairman of ATT which owned the satellite. Telstar could function for only 18 minutes on each two-and-a-half hour orbit, however, when it came into the correct line of sight. Sustained transatlantic broadcasting of a live event was first achieved on 16 May 1963, with the combined use of two satellites, Telstar 1 and Telstar 2, to cover the launch and rescue of astronaut Major Gordon Cooper. By November 1963, such a broadcast would still be a very special event, requiring careful advanced preparation. Television links between Britain and the United States were still in their infancy.

Despite its limitations, Telstar captured the popular imagination. In December 1962, the record of that name by Billy Fury's former backing group, the Tornados, was the first hit by a British band to top the US singles chart. Its space age sound effects were a winning gimmick for a public besotted with technological progress in general and space travel in particular.

**ITV's mid-evening slot from 7.30 was filled by an episode of *Emergency Ward 10* on 22 November. As now, medical dramas proved very popular. The series starred Charles Tingwell, Jill Brownea and Desmond Carrington. *The Hulton-Deutsch Collection Ltd***

the evening with the teenage excitements of *Ready, Steady, Go!*, with its grabbing catch phrase 'The Weekend Starts Here'. On 22 November the top of the bill was Gerry and the Pacemakers, with Freddie and the Dreamers, Kathy Kirby, Kenny Lynch, and the (relatively unknown) Rolling Stones. The programme was not yet introduced by the young and trendy Cathy McGowan, but by the more staid Keith Fordyce. Viewers outside London were mostly denied the thrills of television's hottest pop programme, although Granada had its own alternative, *Scene*, running at the same time.

ITV continued in a style that was very noticeably more populist than the BBC. The schedules for London continued with Michael Miles' game show *Take Your Pick* (featuring the Yes-No Interlude with Alec Dane on the gong), the medical soap *Emergency-Ward 10* and motorized adventure in *Route 66* (most of the regions had the Western series *Bonanza* instead of *Route 66*). After the evening news, Friday Night drama provided some weightier matter with a play by Jack Rosenthal. Standard forensic fare from *Boyd QC* took the schedule up to 10.35, at which time the commercial channels assumed most of their viewers would be going to bed — there were foreign affairs, political reports, and second-rate maritime action in the *Adventures of Seahawk*, up to the *Epilogue* at 11.50.

By midnight British TV screens were blank. Excluding schools television and Welsh programmes, BBC broadcast for only ten hours of the day although this meagre sum was slightly more than ITV managed, even with educational broadcasting included. On the other hand, only one programme scheduled for either channel that evening was a repeat, and there were no movies. It was usual for both channels to show only one film a week, typically on a Sunday afternoon or a Saturday evening. If you wanted to see a movie, you went to the cinema.

A selection of programmes from the rest of the week's viewing provides plenty of nostalgia points: Patrick Macnee and Honor Blackman starring in *The Avengers* on Saturday night; Roger Moore as *The Saint*; *The Beverly Hillbillies*; *No Hiding Place* starring Raymond Francis as Detective Chief Superintendent Lockhart; Patrick Wymark as John Wilder in the *Plane Makers*; *Naked City*; *Big G* with Charles Bronson and Ryan O'Neal; Jack Warner in *Dixon of Dock Green*; *Bonanza*, the Western saga of the Cartwright family; *Wells Fargo*; the ill-fated BBC soap *Compact*; Rupert Davies as *Maigret*; Miriam Karlin and Reg Varney in the *Rag Trade*; Lucille Ball's *The Lucy Show* and Richard Chamberlain in *Dr Kildare*. Any of these will do to evoke the period for those who lived through it in front of the 'tele'.

The influence of television was a

**One of the cult programmes of the era was ABC's *The Avengers*. Two of the programme's stars — Honor Blackman and Patrick MacNee — are seen on the set of the episode entitled 'Brief for Murder'.**
***The Hulton-Deutsch Collection Ltd***

profoundly controversial issue in 1963. The first 'TV generation' was growing up, and there were dire prognostications about the effect the 'goggle box' would prove to have had on everything from their eyesight to their religious belief. In the United States, for example, Newton N. Minow of the Federal Communications Commission had denounced television as a 'vast wasteland', calling for more educational programmes and less violence. In Britain, similar views were commonly expressed in the conservative press; in 1964 Mary Whitehouse would launch her crusade against sex, violence and bad language on the box through her Viewers and Listeners Association.

The endlessly reiterated complaints about sex and violence on television at this time seem very strange, looking back after three more decades of increasingly explicit and gory viewing. The relatively mild programmes of the day had, by the standards of the 1990s, low violence content — shootings in Westerns were bloodless, punches left no trace but a little light bruising, and people were never transmogrified into werewolves or skeletons dripping molten flesh. And sexual censorship was extremely rigorous — no naked bums or breasts, no simulated orgasms, no four-letter words (the public would have to wait another two years for the privilege of hearing the word 'fuck' spo-

**Commonly known as *TW3*, *That Was The Week That Was* brought satire into the 1960s with a vengeance. Rarely pulling its punches, the programme was to launch the career of many of the best known media personalities of the past 30 years, most notably David Frost. Two of the other stars of the programme were Millicent Martin and Lance Percival. *The Hulton-Deutsch Collection Ltd***

ken on television for the first time, by theatre critic Kenneth Tynan).

But the threshold of excitement was far lower in 1963. People had not had their sensibilities blunted by bombardment with input from computer games or video nasties. When *Dr Who*, in an early episode, showed the shadow of a caveman lifting a rock and hurling it down to crush an enemy at his feet, parents were shocked and terrified children watched through their fingers, although there was no blood and the victim was not even seen. *That Was The Week That Was* amazed with the boldness of its open references to sex. Although no sex was shown, the existence of sex, including adultery and homosexuality, was acknowledged, and that was enough to scare a generation that depended on ignorance to keep sexual immorality at bay. Similarly, the 'realistic' language (the use of the word 'bloody', for example) in 'kitchen sink' dramas caused embarrassment and outrage in families where such words, although known to all, had never been openly acknowledged.

In her book *Cleaning Up TV*, Mary Whitehouse described some of the scenes she found most objectionable on television in the early 1960s. These included an episode of *Dr Kildare* in which 'a young woman had been shown in labour. There were close-up shots of her screams and agony...' There was a scene in a play in which 'a man was shown unbuttoning his trousers before getting into bed with a woman (not his wife)'. And especially revolting was a documentary on the future of Britain, shown in the summer of 1963, which included a contribution from sexologist Dr Alex Comfort, who put forward the radical view that 'a chivalrous boy' should be defined as 'one who takes contraceptives with him when he goes to meet his girlfriend'.

For Mrs Whitehouse, this was a 'propaganda of disbelief, doubt and dirt that the BBC projects into millions of homes through the television screen... Crime, violence, illegitimacy and venereal disease are steadily increasing, yet the BBC employs people whose ideas and advice pander to the lowest in human nature and accompany this with a stream of suggestive and erotic plays which present promiscuity, infidelity and drinking [sic] as normal and inevitable.'

Although Mary Whitehouse's obsession with maintaining 'the Christian way of life' — or at least her interpretation of it — was shared by only a small minority in Britain, the eruption of her movement did reveal important tensions in the country's relationship to television. The sort of people who produced television programmes were themselves a small and unrepresentative minority, whose attitudes and instincts were often at odds with — or as they would have said, in advance of — the majority of the population. This sophisticated élite had a conscious, if only half formulated, desire to change the way the population at large thought and felt, particularly about sex, but also about other issues such as race, class and religion. It was a golden age for broadcasters because they could take themselves seriously, without yet having to take seriously the attitudes and opinions of their

## TV Westerns

The early 1960s were the golden age of the TV Western, reflecting straightforward moral values (backed up by righteous violence) and uncomplicated versions of male heroism that were to become increasingly difficult to sustain as the decade advanced. *Bonanza* related the saga of the Cartwright family at Ponderosa Ranch, with Lorne Greene as the grizzled Ben, Michael Landon as Little Joe and the lovably sloth-brained Hoss played by Dan Blocker. *Wagon Train* rattled its cast of standard character types weekly westward. *Wells Fargo* starred Dale Robertson as special agent Jim Hardie. And *Rawhide*, the tale of a seemingly endless, seriously accident-prone cattle drive to Kansas, rode high on its catchphrase, 'Git 'em up...move 'em out', and its theme tune sung by Frankie Laine. The most charismatic of the cowpokes — though not topping the credits — was Rowdy Yates, alias Clint Eastwood. In late 1963, Eastwood's career was making so little progress that he would soon agree to star in the most unlikely of downmarket projects, an Italian Western: Sergio Leone's *Per un Pugno di Dollari*.

***Top:*** **Westerns were among the most popular TV genres of the early 1960s. Shows included *Bonanza, Rawhide and Wagon Train. The Hulton-Deutsch Collection Ltd***

***Above:*** **Starring Clint Eastwood, *Rawhide* was a tale of driving cattle to Kansas. It also featured Nine Shipman, Jamie Best and Denver Pyle but only Eastwood was to burst through and achieve super-stardom through his roles in the various Spaghetti Westerns directed by Sergio Leone — *For a Fistful of Dollars* and *For a Few Dollars More. The Hulton-Deutsch Collection Ltd***

## Route 66

One of the most successful TV series of the early 1960s, *Route 66* was above all a celebration of a car: the Chevrolet Corvette. Then America's only native sports car, the Corvette stood for escapism, excitement and pure adventure. It was the car of every young American's dreams — though very few could afford the $4,000 price tag. They could, however, live the Corvette experience vicariously through *Route 66*.

Each week the program's two easy-going heroes roamed the backroads of the American heartland, solving a crisis or two and always moving on. As David Barry wrote in his study of the American love affair with the automobile, *Street Dreams,* 'The image of a red Corvette pounding down a two-lane blacktop to the driving jazz beat of the *Route 66* theme crystallized a vision of romantic highway wandering that had been part of the American dream since the beginning.'

Incidentally, the title of the programme was not taken directly from the highway that crosses the United States from Chicago to Los Angeles, but from the song 'Route 66' written by Bobby Troupe in the 1940s — a memorable evocation of the thrill of the open road.

viewers. The mounting white discontent with immigration, for example, was exposed, denounced, scorned, lampooned and preached against, but the concerns behind it were never addressed.

One factor always neglected in the raging debate over the impact of television was the effect of the actual conditions under which the box was watched. Unlike cinema, television was a family experience, and a family experience with the lights on. In 1963, there were very likely to be three generations viewing in the same room, because there would only be one television in a house and more extended families lived together. And these three generations were steeped in a culture of hypocrisy and repression, in which more things were left unspoken between parents and children than would now seem conceivable. No wonder, then, that sex and bad language brought more complaints than violence on screen: the cause was sheer embarrassment.

If a woman was young and stylish, whether in Britain or the United States, on 22 November 1963 she was very likely to be wearing clothes from the Mary Quant range. With her husband Alexander Plunkett-Green, Quant had opened her first boutique, Bazaar, on the King's Road in Chelsea in 1955. By 1963 she had gone into wholesale distribution and her clothes were being sold in 150 shops in the UK and double that number in the United States.

Mary Quant styles epitomised the bold,

## That Was The Week That Was

On the evening of 22 November, the cast of the BBC's Saturday late night satire show *That Was The Week That Was* were assembled at the Dorchester Hotel in London for the Television Producers and Directors Guild awards ceremony, in which they were to feature prominently as one of the outstanding TV hits of 1963. But the one-year-old programme was not destined to get much older. The previous week, on 13 November, the BBC governors had decided to take *That Was The Week That Was* off the air at the end of the year, despite a weekly audience of 12 million. Although the satirist had the wholehearted support of the BBC's iconoclastic director-general Sir Hugh Carlton Greene, the vice-chairman, Sir James Duff, had threatened to resign if it continued.

*TW3*, as it was labelled for convenience, had grown out of the early 1960s satire boom. The revue *Beyond the Fringe*, with Alan Bennett, Dudley Moore, Peter Cook and Jonathan Miller, had taken irreverent Oxbridge undergraduate humour onto a world stage: by 1963, it was playing to enthusiastic audiences in New York. Another product of the time was the magazine *Private Eye*, produced by Richard Ingrams, Christopher Booker and William Rushton. Sir Hugh Greene wanted to bring

*Left:* **On the set of *That Was The Week That Was*. It was the first programme to display the cameras, lights and other clutter of an early 1960s TV studio as a feature of the show. *The Hulton-Deutsch Collection Ltd***

***Bottom: That Was The Week That Was* helped establish the careers of many well-known performers. These included, Lance Percival and Willie Rushton, left, David Frost, standing in the centre, later fronting a version of the show on American television. *The Hulton-Deutsch Collection Ltd***

this mildly subversive anti-establishment fun to television, despite the long-standing BBC rule that humour should never touch on the four sacred subjects: politics, religion, royalty and sex. Officially categorized as Current Affairs rather than Light Entertainment, *TW3* was able to drive a bulldozer through this ruling, creating a gap that others have poured through ever since

Produced by Ned Sherrin, the programme was fronted by the youthful David Frost. It opened with Millicent Martin singing 'That was the week that was. It's over, let it go.' Lance Percival improvised topical calypsos on subjects suggested by the studio audience. Bernard Levin tore a studio guest to shreds each week with an astonishingly vitriolic interview technique — which never stopped other victims presenting themselves for slaughter. There was also William Rushton, especially good as Macmillan; Timothy Birdsall cartooning on stage; and, among others, Eleanor Bronn, Roy Kinnear, John Wells, John Bird and Roy Hudd. This collective talent, backed up by writing from the likes of Keith Waterhouse, John Mortimer, Dennis Potter and Kenneth Tynan, guaranteed more hits than misses in the hastily rehearsed sketches.

The programme was technically innovative, being the first show to allow the studio to appear in full view, cameras and all. But it was the content of the sketches that caused a sensation. The satire on political figures such as the home secretary, Henry Brooke, and Prime Minister Sir Alec Douglas-Home was merciless. The 19 October address to Home provoked 600 phone calls and 300 letters of complaint. Religion was also fair game: much offense was caused by a consumer's guide — 'This handy little faith [Anglicanism]... if you want transubstantiation you can have it, if you don't you don't have to... ', and so on. And then there were tacky jokes about sex, a useful line of criticism for Conservative MPs who did not want to admit that what they really hated was the satire.

*TW3* drove its enemies to a fury. One critic denounced Sherrin and Frost as 'pedlars of filth and smut and destroyers of all that Britain holds dear'. A vicar, writing in his parish magazine, described Bernard Levin abusively as a 'thick-lipped Jewboy'. Questions were asked in the House of Commons; bishops fulminated from their pulpits.

The excuse finally given for closing down *TW3* was that it coud not be guaranteed to give balanced political coverage during an election year. The real reason was that it had proved just too hot to handle.

**Mary Quant — one of the gurus of early 1960s fashion.** ***The Hulton-Deutsch Collection Ltd***

## DR WHO

One group of individuals feeling a special excitement on 22 November were the producer, writers and actors of a new BBC science fiction drama series, *Dr Who,* which was due to broadcast its first episode at 5.15 p.m. the following day.

Fifty-two episodes of *Dr Who* were planned to fill the Saturday evening slot between *Grandstand* and *Juke Box Jury* for the next year, but top executives at the BBC had little confidence in the series and were fearful of a flop. Both for Sydney Newman, BBC Head of Drama since the start of the year, and the series producer, Verity Lambert, who was producing her first programme, a lot was riding on *Dr Who*'s success.

Entitled 'An Unearthly Child', the first episode was written by Anthony Coburn and introduced the original cast of four time travellers: William Hartnell as the Doctor, William Russell and Jacqueline Hill as the teachers Ian and Barbara, and Carole Ann Ford as the Doctor's grand-daughter, Susan. The Tardis time machine, disguised as a police box, is discovered in a junk yard a standard TV location of the time, as in Steptoe and Son. The two teachers, intrigued by their strange pupil Susan, get inside the Tardis and are, in effect, kidnapped by the Doctor, who whisks them off to 100,000 bc.

The first episode was originally scheduled to be shown on 16 November, but was delayed for a week by production difficulties. Overshadowed by the Kennedy assassination, the broadcast on 23 November passed almost unnoticed. The series was rescued by the decision to repeat episode 1 immediately before episode 2 the following week. An audience of almost 6 million saw the repeat and critical response was favourable. Early in 1964, the Daleks would arrive to raise the series to cult status.

youthful frivolity of the time. According to *Vogue*, Quant had 'discovered what no one in England knew - there was a whole new want among bright, young English girls for new, young, skinny clothes that sometimes have the look of fancy dress.' Instead of the sophisticated, expensive chic styles traditionally peddled by the Parisian fashion houses, she created clothes that were simple, sometimes ridiculous, but always fun. It was up-to-the-minute fashion for the young at prices they could afford. 'I had always wanted young people to have a fashion of their own, absolutely Twentieth Century fashion,' she later wrote. 'The young were tired of wearing essentially the same as their mothers.'

In the autumn of 1963, Quant had launched her Ginger Group label, based on the mix-and-match principle — all the elements of clothing, accessories and make-up fitted together in an all-over 'look'. This was mass-market style, a democratisation of the fashion tradition that had previously traded on exclusivity and élitism. The chic Parisian fashion house, Pierre Cardin, had also just launched an off-the-peg range of mass-produced clothing. From now on, style was for everyone. And if women couldn't afford to buy the clothes in the shops, there was a flourishing market in Mary Quant patterns to be knitted or made up at home.

The women's style of 1963 was angular,

## POLICE BOX

Later generations of *Dr Who* fans may have been puzzled by the Tardis's outer shape, a blue Police Box, seeming as unreal as any other aspect of the series. But in 1963 there were over 600 of these strange objects on the streets of London and many more in provincial cities.

The main function of the Police Box was to keep the copper on the beat in touch with headquarters, before the days of portable two-way radios. A blue light on top of the box would flash to attract a patrolling policeman's attention when there was a message for him from his station. Inside the box was a telephone, which the public were also entitled to use in an emergency.

Police Boxes disappeared from the London streets in 1969, but thanks to *Dr Who*, more than two decades later one at least was still voyaging across the space-time continuum.

## American Cars

In 1963, designers within the American car industry were feeling for a route away from the fin and chrome-laden monsters that had powered their way along the highways of the previous decade. Americans had grown to expect a car to combine a massively powerful gas-guzzling engine with the comfort of a living room and the tastefulness of an amusement park. It would still be some years before small foreign cars began to make a dent in sales of Cadillacs, Chryslers, Chevrolets and Plymouths.

Probably the most stylish car of 1963 in the United States was the Buick Riviera, which blended luxury and power with more restrained and elegant lines. The fastest was almost certainly the Shelby AC Cobra, a small car with a high-powered engine on a lightweight British sports car chassis. And the most desirable was possibly the 1963 Corvette Sting Ray, a vehicle with a more sophisticated style but a less crudely adventurous image than the early 1960s model Corvette used in the TV program *Route 66*.

THE MOTOR October 16 1963

**1964 GALAXIE 500** The Galaxies have swept the board in Saloon Car Racing this Season—superb performance in luxury.

**1964 FAIRLANE 500** North American feel and performance in convenient size.

**FORD FOR 1964-BRED IN COMPETITION BUILT FOR TOTAL PERFORMANCE**

These beautiful Right Hand Drive Canadian Fords have so much to offer —
The silky power of V8 Engines, Automatic Transmission, Luxury Seating for six—and of course power assisted Brakes and Steering (on the Galaxie)
Competition bred, these cars have really outstanding, effortless performance.

Ford

**YOU WILL FEEL THE DIFFERENCE WHEN YOU DRIVE THEM**

Please ask for a test drive or call at-
**LINCOLN CARS LTD.**
OR YOUR NEAREST CANADIAN FORD DEALER
GREAT WEST RD · BRENTFORD
MIDDLESEX · ISLEWORTH 6071

THE MOTOR October 16 1963



# ROVER 1964

Rover moves into 1964 with a range of superb cars. Cars renowned for Rover engineering. Rover performance. Rover luxury. Leading is the advanced Rover 2000—highlight of this year's Motor Show. With it, the Rover 3-Litre Saloon Mark II and the Coupé. And, of course, the Rover 110 and 95.

**Rover—one of the world's best engineered cars**

THE ROVER COMPANY LIMITED, SOLIHULL, WARWICKSHIRE
London offices and showrooms: Devonshire House, Piccadilly. *Makers of fine cars and the world-famous Land-Rover*

***Above:*** **A month before Kennedy's death, the Motor Show was held at Earls Court in London. North American Ford, through its Lincoln Cars Ltd subsidiary, attempted to launch two of its successful American cars into the British market. The Ford Galaxie 500 was priced at £1,700 basic — a contrast to the more usual £425 basic price of the Ford Anglia or the £474 of the Cortina.** ***The Motor***

***Left:*** **In 1963 one of the great names of British motoring was Rover — just as it is 30 years later. But, in the early 1960s, the company was still an independent force; the traumas of the British Leyland era were yet to happen. The Rover 2000, unveiled at the show, was destined to become a classic car of its generation. All yours for only £1,046 (basic) in 1963.** ***The Motor***

*Right:* **The great new fabric for the autumn of 1963 was Bri-Nylon. According to the publicity at the time 'The thick bulky textures and casual lines will emphasise the muffled wrapped-up silhouettes which Paris stressed so strongly .... it is a practical "wash and wear" for the single girls and bachelor boys, to change into their best everyday, plus a wide colour range for eye-catching appeal'.** ***The Hulton-Deutsch Collection Ltd***

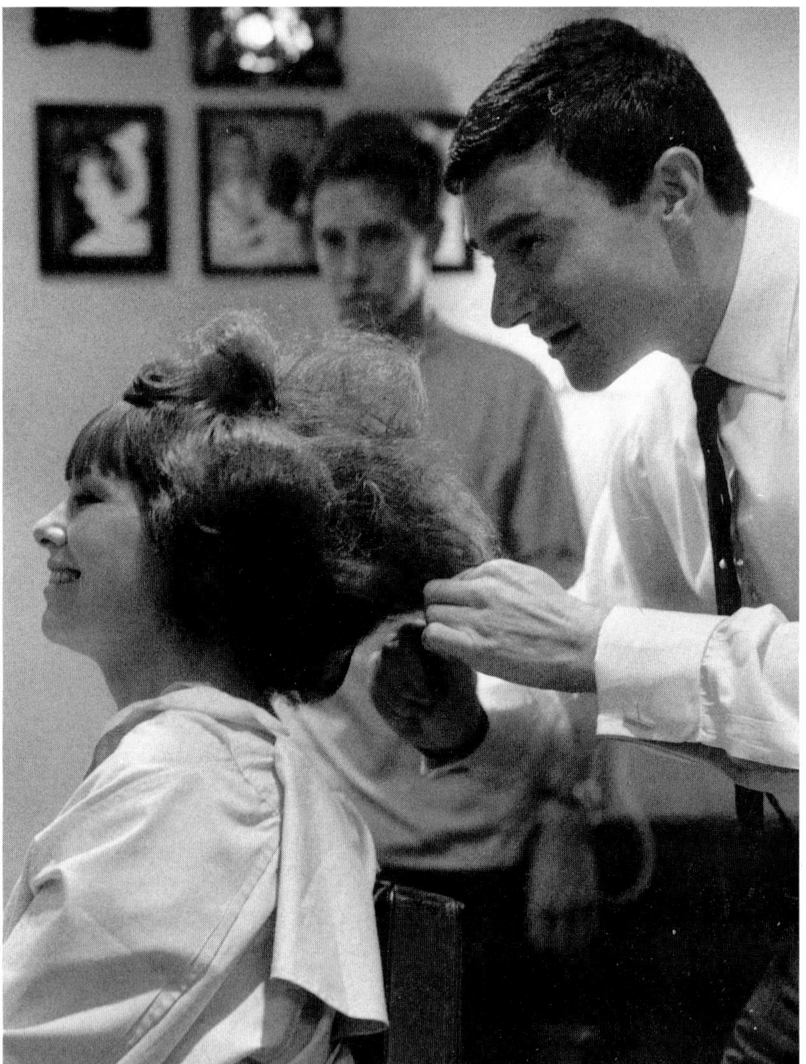

*Below:* **If Mary Quant was setting the standards for fashion design, then Vidal Sassoon was doing the same for hair.** ***The Hulton-Deutsch Collection Ltd***

with bold clean lines that ignored the contours of the female body. The shift to the pinafore and the sackdress abolished the waistline and the curvaceous hips that had defined feminine looks for so long. The new styles gave women a childlike look — irreverent and fun-loving, but sexually docile and unthreatening. The new breed of fashion models underlined this effect of wilful immaturity and passivity with their skinny, gangling legginess. The recently discovered French pop idol Françoise Hardy was *Vogue*'s favourite icon for the year, with her lithe unaffected student look. In Britain, Jean Shrimpton reigned with what *Vogue* described as her 'extraordinary fragility and delicacy of body'.

Newly fashionable hairdresser Vidal Sassoon had produced the haircut to match the Quant look — 'the Bob', a short, chunky, provocatively geometrical style. If a woman did not have the hair to suit, she could always wear a wig. Artificial hair was definitely in, and a remarkable number of women through the 1960s would have a hairpiece or two in their wardrobe.

Nineteen sixty-three was the year in which hemlines began the inexorable rise that was to end with designer John Bates' boast of the 'Smallest Dress in the World' two years later. This was not yet the era of the mini-skirt, but hemlines an inch above the knee seemed provocative enough at the time, leading one contemporary commentator to christen 1963 'the Year of the Leg'. Breasts were now kept well covered and a cleavage was unthinkably styleless and old-fashioned.

Short skirts and dresses went with patterned stockings or boots of all varieties — the Parisian designer Courrèges had a big hit with boots of white kidskin. As yet there were no tights, which was to prove a problem as hemlines rose. Necessity eventually proved the mother of invention, but for a while short hemlines went with stockings and suspenders. The period between the adoption of the mini skirt and the introduction of tights was the golden age of the voyeur on the escalator.

Carnaby Street, a dingy backstreet of Victorian warehouses on the edge of Soho, was just emerging as a focus of youth fashion shopping. Sally Tuffin and Marion Foale, two graduates of the Royal College of Art, had set up shop there in 1961 and developed a flourishing trade in 'fun' clothes. John Stephen had also arrived and was almost taking over the street, such was the demand for his trendy Mod male fashion.

The Mods were the leading faction in the youth style wars of the early 1960s. As Mary Quant wrote: 'It was the Mods who gave the dress trade the impetus to break through the fast moving, breathtaking, uprooting revolution.' The name was originally applied to a trendy London clique devoted to stylish male clothing and modern jazz (hence 'Mod'). By the end of 1963, it denoted rhythm and blues fans who rode scooters and popped Purple Hearts. The common link between these two avatars of the Mod was a concentration on men, rather than women, as the focus of fashion concerns. Cathy McGowan commented at the time that 'the Mod boys are getting prettier and prettier, while the girls get plainer and plainer.'

According to McGowan, herself a Mod, the Mods of November 1963 lived in 'a cool

**The era before compulsory crash helmets — a group of Mods parade along the sea front at Hastings under the watchful presence of a bemused police constable. The early 1960s were marked by regular confrontations, particularly at Bank Holidays, between Mods and Rockers at the popular seaside resorts.**
***The Hulton-Deutsch Collection Ltd***

## STYLISH MODS AND STYLELESS ROCKERS

Cathy McGowan, *Ready, Steady, Go!* presenter and 'Queen of the Mods', offered her own version of the 'whacky, with-it world of Rockers and Mods' in the *TV Times* in December 1963. Her biassed description not only gives a snapshot of youth fashions at the time, but also conveys a sense of the natural antagonism between the bikers and the denizens of Carnaby Street.

'Right now the boys are wearing brightly coloured shirts... Their slim-line trousers are dark, half-mast. French-style casual shoes are in. Hair styles are short, all-one-length and parted mostly in the middle.

'Definitely out for boys: back-combed hair and hair lacquer. But important status symbols are suede jackets with leather collars, or shortie, Peter Pan style overcoats...

'The Mod girl is bang in fashion at the moment if she wears a simple crew-neck sweater... a plain straight grey skirt, worn an inch above the knee, with knee-length wool socks to match the sweater worn over white nylons... The Mod girl wears no make-up, except heavy eye shadow and hair in the Cleopatra, eyebrow-length fringe style.

'Definitely out for girls: back-combing, bright colours and plastic hand-bags...'

To the Queen of Mod, the bike-worshipping Rockers looked Neanderthal: 'They have little fashion taste,' she sneers. 'The boys wear tight jeans, black leather jerkins with vivid emblems on the back, and clod-hopping flying boots.

'The girls like tight black skirts, clinging sweaters, and masses of make-up. They wear their hair in long Bardot styles and still wear black patterned nylons...

'Rockers are still doing the Twist (which went out two years ago) and idolise Elvis Presley, who is desperately old fashioned...'

world of fashion, scooters and way-out dances' (one current dance craze was the Hitler, performed with the right arm raised for the Nazi salute). Their stylishness depended on the new-found prosperity of youth. According to McGowan, the average Mod would spend at least £5 a week on clothes and accessories, plus the cost of the clubs, coffee bars and steak houses where they paraded themselves, and the inevitable scooter. 'The Mod has no real ambition,' McGowan wrote, 'except to earn enough money to continue to be fashionable...'

The natural enemies of the Mods were the Rockers, unreformed bikers who lived off a diet of beer and egg-and-chips, put Brylcream on their hair, and had neither class nor money. According to McGowan, 'Mods are the fashion-conscious, with-it teenagers; Rockers are the old-fashioned ton-up kids who think more of motor bikes than themselves.' At Easter 1964 the antagonism between Mods and Rockers was to break out into notorious riots at British seaside resorts.

For the cultured élite, that Friday evening in London offered some choice attractions. At the Royal Ballet, Margot Fonteyn and Rudolph Nureyev were dancing in Frederick Ashton's *Marguerite and Armand*. At the Royal Festival Hall, Benjamin Britten's opera *Gloriana* was being given a concert performance in honour of the composer's 50th birthday, with Peter Pears singing the part of the Earl of Essex. And at the Old Vic, a production of Chekhov's *Uncle Vanya*, directed by Laurence Olivier, and starring Joan Plowright and Sir Michael Redgrave, had just opened to rave reviews.

*Uncle Vanya* was the second production by the newly formed National Theatre Company. It had recorded its first performance in October, almost 60 years after such an institution had first been proposed, with an uncut version of *Hamlet*, also directed by Laurence Olivier, and starring Peter O'Toole in the leading rôle. As yet the National Theatre itself was still to be built, but on the morning of 22 November it was announced that the architect for the new building would be Denys Lasdun. British drama seemed on the verge of a renaissance. In New York, the critical success of the season was Albert Finney in John Osborne's *Luther*, directed by Tony Richardson. Finney, who had also starred in Richardson's Oscar-winning film *Tom Jones*, was at the peak of his fame, especially in the United States. *Newsweek* had run a cover feature on Finney at the end of October, bracketing him with O'Toole, Richard Harris, Alan Bates and Tom Courtenay as part of a lively new generation that was replacing the elegant suavity of Olivier and Gielgud with a fresher, tougher style.

Finney and Courtenay, in particular, were associated with the gritty social realism of British films in the early 1960s, such as Tony Richardson's *A Taste of Honey* (starring Rita Tushingham as a pregnant and unmarried waif), Karl Reisz's version of Alan Sillitoe's novel *Saturday Night and Sunday Morning*, John Schlesinger's *A Kind of Loving* and *Billy Liar* (also starring new discovery Julie Christie) and Lindsay Anderson's *This Sporting Life*. Shot in black-and-white on location in the industrial north of England, they showed would-be rebels trapped by the frustrating limitations and hypocrisies of provincial working class life. With their moody jazz

**The ballet stars Rudolf Nureyev and Margot Fonteyn were at their peak in the early 1960s. They are seen here rehearsing *Marguerite and Armand* at Covent Garden in March 1963. *The Hulton-Deutsch Collection Ltd***

scores and often daringly sexual themes, these kitchen-sink movies were a popular as well as an artistic success. But British cinema had moved into the big time when it took on some American finance and switched to colour and fantasy. The result was *Tom Jones,* the biggest movie hit of 1963 both in Britain and the United States.

*Tom Jones* was one of three internationally successful British films showing in London on 22 November. The others were David Lean's epic *Lawrence of Arabia* and the second James Bond movie, *From Russia With Love*. The Bond movies, based on Ian Fleming's best-selling novels, had begun in 1962 with the relatively low-budget *Dr No*, which climbed to be a popular success unhyped. This was followed in 1963 by *From Russia With Love,* and by November Bond was a craze in Britain second only to the Beatles. (President Kennedy listed *From Russia With Love* among his top ten favourite books.)

The Bond movies encapsulated many of the obsessions of the time: glossy sex, technological gimmickry, espionage, and cool affectless violence. Their charismatic

**Another of the great artistic double acts of the 1960s was that of the composer Benjamin Britten (seen here seated) and the tenor Peter Pears (standing). Britten's 50th birthday was being celebrated on the evening of 22 November at the Royal Festival Hall. *The Hulton-Deutsch Collection Ltd***

*Above:* **Directed by Tony Richardson, *A Taste of Honey* was a version of Shelagh Delaney's play. It starred Rita Tushingham, Dora Bryan, Robert Stephens and Murray Melvin. The story of a Salford girl leaving home and becoming pregnant was mildly shocking at the time in its sympathetic portrayal of single parenthood and homosexuality.** ***BFI Stills, Posters and Designs***

*Right:* **Based on the character created by Keith Waterhouse, *Billy Liar* was directed by John Schlesinger (who was later to achieve fame in Hollywood as the director of *Midnight Cowboy*). It starred Tom Courtenay as its eponymous hero — a northern undertaker's clerk who escapes from his mundane existence through fantasy.** ***BFI Stills, Posters and Designs***

*Left:* John Schlesinger's first feature was *A Kind of Loving* which starred Alan Bates as a man trapped into marriage with June Ritchie through an unplanned pregnancy. The film was typical of the British 'New Wave' of the era, featuring life at the raw end in a northern factory environment. *BFI Stills, Posters and Designs*

*Below:* Karel Reisz's *Saturday Night and Sunday Morning* starred Albert Finney as a Nottingham factory worker who rejects the limited horizons offered by his working class upbringing. Determined to take whatever he can, irrespective of the consequences, he is ultimately destined to fail. The film was famous for originating the phrase 'Don't let the bastards grind you down' — a sentence that was to have a considerable impact 30 years later. *BFI Stills, Posters and Designs*

**In 1963 the second James Bond film, *From Russia with Love*, was released. Starring Sean Connery,seen here in early 1963, in the role for which he became best-known, the film helped to create the reputation of the James Bond films for dramatic action sequences. *The Hulton-Deutsch Collection Ltd***

star Sean Connery projected many of the qualities foreigners traditionally liked to associate with the British — an exaggerated coolness under pressure, an ironic wit in the face of danger — but his behaviour was definitely not cricket. Bond was amoral in relation to women and to killing; the movies were a slick fantasy with no moral content at all. The message of the popular response to the early Bond films was that people were tired of worthy self-righteousness. They wanted sex and violence to be fun.

The film industry was happy to find anything that would induce people to desert their televisions for the cinema. The drop in cinema attendances worldwide was threatening the very existence of Hollywood. The figures for Britain can be taken as typical: in 1953, there had been 1,284 million movie tickets sold; ten years later, the figure was 357 million — a drop of more than 900 million in a decade. The movie moguls guessed the answer was to give people what they couldn't get on television at home. The first obvious solution lay in size and colour: the early 1960s were the high water mark of the wide screen epic.

But this was a risky strategy. Joseph Mankiewicz's *Cleopatra*, still showing on its first run in London in November 1963, had taken four years to shoot and cost $40 million, making it then the most expensive movie ever. The expense nearly sank Twentieth Century Fox. During the production, the film's female lead, Elizabeth Taylor, had barely survived a potentially fatal illness, divorced her fourth husband, Eddie Fisher, and started an affair with her future fifth, co-star Richard Burton. Yet despite the helpful publicity surrounding these events, Cleopatra, an opulent but dull movie, was hardly a runaway success.

Many of the best movies on show in November 1963 were made in black and white, largely to cut costs, but also as an aesthetic reaction against the vulgarity of wide screen colour. One example was Federico Fellini's 8 ½, in part a satire on the elephantine state of contemporary movie making, in part a demonstration of how a masterly director could still use the overblown medium to express his most personal fantasies and obsessions. Other current examples were Hitchcock's paranoid masterpiece *The Birds;* a film called *Knife in the Water* by a Polish newcomer, Roman Polanski; Orson Welles's version of Kafka's *The Trial*; and Joseph Losey's *The Servant*, starring Dirk Bogarde, James Fox and Sarah Miles, with a darkly comic script by Harold Pinter.

The most inescapable actress of the

year was Claudia Cardinale, who could be seen with Peter Sellers in the first of the *Pink Panther* movies, in Fellini's *8 ½*, and in Luchino Visconti's *The Leopard*, with Burt Lancaster and Alain Delon. Worst actress of the year, at least according to the *Harvard Lampoon*, was the young Jane Fonda for her part in the dreadful flop *In the Cool of the Day*. Worst film of the year was probably *It's A Mad, Mad, Mad, Mad World*, an epic comedy as overblown as its title.

The best choice for the filmgoer on 22 November would certainly have been a European or British movie, rather than any Hollywood product on offer. Hollywood would learn the lesson later by allowing more individual freedom to its directors and more challenging subject-matter on to the screen.

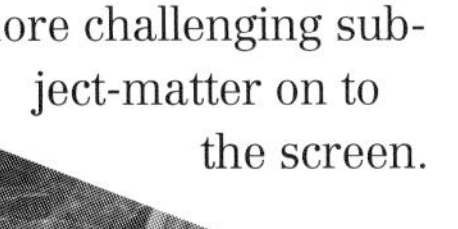

***Left:*** **The queue for an early performance of *Cleopatra*. *BFI Stills, Posters and Designs***

***Above:*** **At more than four hours in length, Joseph Mankiewicz's *Cleopatra* could lay claim to being the blockbusting epic of 1963. But to many, it earned its reputation as the start of the tempestuous relationship between the film's two stars — Elizabeth Taylor and Richard Burton. *BFI Stills, Posters and Designs***

***Left:*** **Following their appearance together in *Cleopatra*, Richard Burton and Elizabeth Taylor also featured in the *Night of 100 Stars* at the London Palladium. The pair are seen in typical July weather in London as Burton struggles with his umbrella. *The Hulton-Deutsch Collection Ltd***

The year 1963 has become especially associated with sex because of a piece of doggerel by British poet Phillip Larkin, written later in the decade:

Sexual intercourse began
In nineteen sixty-three
(Which was rather late for me)
Between the end of the Chatterley ban
And the Beatles' first LP.

Sexual freedom was an issue of the moment. Everyone was convinced that, whether they advocated it or disapproved of it, some form of sexual revolution was taking place. Exactly what shape this revolution was taking, or should take, or would take if it was not prevented, was totally unclear. But radicals and conservatives had drawn up their motley ranks on opposite sides of this divide and battle was joined.

In particular, the contraceptive Pill, authorized for sale at the start of the decade, and the less-often mentioned IUDs had opened up expectations of a tide of promiscuity — although no form of contraception except the traditional sheath was widely used in 1963. Whether the sexual behaviour of the young in 1963 was in fact any different from that of their elders a decade or two earlier is hard to establish. In November 1963, for example, *Newsweek* was running a series of articles on the sex life of American students. The interest was provoked by a statement from the dean of Harvard College, John U. Monro, that the male students' privilege of entertaining women in their rooms had 'come to be considered a license to use the college rooms for wild parties or for sexual intercourse'. However, examining the details of the case, a modern student might be startled to find that the Harvard men's 'privilege' was fixed between 4 p.m. and 7 p.m. each day; outside these hours, female visitors were strictly forbidden. Other American universities were even less liberal: Columbia allowed its students women guests only on alternate Sundays, and Boston allowed no visits at all.

A psychiatrist, Graham B. Blaine Jr., wheeled out to comment on the controversy, suggested that more college boys than in previous generations were 'having intercourse with the girls they date rather than with prostitutes or pick-ups.'

## UNDERGROUND CINEMA

Cinema fans in New York looking for something completely different could savour the questionable delights of the newly burgeoning underground movie scene, promoted by Jonas Mekas' Film-Maker's Cooperative.

These films were exhibited outside the net of official censorship, and so were able to address sexual — most often homosexual — themes banned from normal cinemas. They were also, however, made in opposition to the generally accepted aesthetic of the cinema. They had no plots, no dialogue or characters in any conventional sense, and were made in a deliberately amateurish manner — poor lighting, out of focus camera, badly framed shots, sound out of sync, and so on. The result was a challenge to Hollywood that had a certain fascination, but was also intensely boring.

Circulating through the underground in November 1963 were Kenneth Anger's *Scorpio Rising*, a homoerotic bike movie with heavy symbolic overtones, Jack Smith's transvestite fantasy *Flaming Creatures*, and Andy Warhol's *Sleep*, a six-hour film of a man asleep. The chief excitement of these movies was the chance that they might at any moment be seized in a police raid — which they often were.

Just as in Britain, Western Europe witnessed a golden age of art house cinema in this period. Amongst the classic films to be released in 1963 was Federico Fellini's *8½*. The director (right) is seen with the film's star Marcello Mastroianna. *The Hulton-Deutsch Collection Ltd*

*Left:* Directed by the 34-year old Kenneth Anger, *Scorpio Rising* was one of the most notorious films of the year. Anger, was later to achive fame as the author of *Hollywood Babylon* — an exposé of scandals from Tinseltown. *BFI Stills, Posters and Designs*

*Below:* Jack Smith's Flaming Creatures; a wild transvestite fantasy, was pursued by the authorities after its underground showing in a Manhattan warehouse. *BFI Stills, Posters and Designs*

He attributed this partly to the 'improvement in contraceptive techniques'. Yet college clinics would only provide contraceptives to unmarried students under what were described as 'special circumstances'.

The family institution was holding together relatively well. In Britain there were 27,000 divorces granted in 1963; by 1990 the figure was 168,000. The United States was noted for its high divorce rate, with 428,000 divorces in 1963, but even that high figure is well below current levels. The relatively low divorce rate meant that many extremely unhappy couples were sharing the same yoke, however. Britain had no arrangement for divorce by mutual consent, and couples still indulged in the archaic procedure of having the husband feign an infidelity, with a private detective

## Tom Jones

Despite superficial appearances, *Tom Jones* was a direct offshot of the gritty realist school. Its screenplay was by John Osborne, whose play *Look Back in Anger* had created the kitchen-sink genre, and its director Tony Richardson and star Albert Finney were both rooted in the cinema of working class revolt. What *Tom Jones* did was to transfer the same raunchy rebel Finney had played in *Saturday Night Sunday Morning* to the more liberated setting of a fantasy 18th century and a wide colour screen.

Tom Jones established British cinema at a peak of international commercial prestige it had never matched before, and has not since. Even before Beatlemania crossed the Atlantic, cinema set the fad for all things British in the United States. *Lawrence of Arabia*, David Lean's desert epic starring Peter O'Toole, had already won its Oscars. The next in line to create an international sensation was James Bond.

**Directed by Tony Richardson, the John Osborne-scripted film of the 18th century classic *Tom Jones* was financed by United Artists from America as it proved impossible to obtain support from Britain. It starred Diane Cilento (above)...**

**...and Albert Finney (left). *The Hulton-Deutsch Collection Ltd (both)***

conveniently present as observer, to provide grounds for a divorce to be approved.

The same ambivalence surrounds the figures for illegitimate births. In Britain 6.6 per cent of births were outside wedlock in 1963 — the United States figure was even lower — compared with 28 per cent in 1990. But how many shotgun weddings and miserable backstreet abortions did the relatively low 1963 statistic reflect?

Whatever was happening in real life, something was definitely happening to the representation of sex in visual images and on the printed page. Here the Western world stood on the brink of a revolution which, in the words of critic Natasha Walter, was to make 'what was once the other world, the underworld of culture — pornography, obscenity and violence — our mainstream.'

Books were in the forefront. Despite the lifting of the ban on D. H. Lawrence's *Lady Chatterley's Lover* in 1960, the battle against censorship continued, with the elegantly pornographic eighteenth-century novel *Fanny Hill* in the firing line. This work was published in paperback in 1963, only to be banned as obscene in both Britain and the United States. But the more crudely descriptive of Henry Miller's novels were emerging into the light, as were the narcotically induced necrophiliac fantasies of William Burroughs in the *Naked Lunch*, and Frank Harris's long suppressed erotic memoirs, *My Life and Loves*. Perhaps more significantly, the mainstream fiction bestseller of November 1963, Mary McCarthy's *The Group*, had as its most hilarious comic setpiece a scene in which a girl struggles with the mysteries of a contraceptive device she mistakenly refers to as a 'peccary'.

In 1963, such freedoms were not permitted on the stage or the screen. Films throughout the world were subject to strict censorship by the authorities, as well as self-censorship by the major movie producers and distributers. Although on 22 November there were cinemas in London showing films with titles like *She Got What She Asked For* and *Nudes of the World*, the actual content of any legitimately screened material was, by the standards of even a decade later, remarkably tame. Even in X-rated movies nudity had to be suggested rather than shown — a back view down to the waist was ultimately risque. Depictions of sex were vague, with much use of the time-honoured fade or dissolve well before any climax. 'Continental' movies, with stars such as Brigitte Bardot and Jeanne Moreau, were noted for being more daring, but hardly went beyond an occasional bare buttock and close-ups of faces exhibiting the lineaments of desire. Most of the explicit sex in movie houses of the early 1960s happened in the back row of the stalls.

In November 1963, authorities throughout the Western world were preoccupied by the rising tide of crime. Yet in retrospect it seems that life was extraordinarily safe. In Britain, for example, on any day in the 1990s an individual is almost six times more likely to be the victim of a crime than they would have been on the day of Kennedy's assassination. In 1963 there were 153 murders in England and Wales, compared with 694 in 1991; 422 reported rapes as against over 4,000 a year in the 1990s; and less than one million crimes in total, compared with 51/4 million in 1991. There is great uncertainty surrounding crime figures — rape was certainly more common in the 1960s than the low statistics would indicate, for example, because many women either accepted enforced sex as one of life's occasional misfortunes or were discouraged from reporting it by the attitude of the police. But there is no doubt that people walked the streets with less fear.

And yet crime figures were already rising steeply in 1963 from the very low levels of earlier decades of the 20th century, and organized crime was a specially high-profile issue in the United States. The war against the mafia was the major theme of Robert Kennedy's tenure as US Attorney-General. Even FBI chief J. Edgar Hoover, who had for so long denied the existence of organized crime in the United States and resisted attempts to investigate it, had belatedly been obliged to devote resources to this non-communist 'enemy within'. In



**The decision of the jury at the famous Old Bailey trial that D. H. Lawrence's *Lady Chatterley's Lover* was not obscene was a landmark in the gradual liberalisation of Britain, helping to usher in the more relaxed attitudes of the 1960s. Priced at 3s 6d (17.5p), the book's staid jacket was typical of the era.**
***The Hulton-Deutsch Collection Ltd***



**There were, however, still attempts to roll back the liberal bandwagon. In December 1963 it was reported that, whilst a copy of the 1893 edition of *Memoirs of a Woman of Pleasure (Fanny Hill)* had been sold at a Christies' auction for £11, a London book distributor was to be prosecuted in January for selling a paperback edition of the same book.**
***The Hulton-Deutsch Collection Ltd***

1960, the last year of the Eisenhower administration, there had been just 19 indictments of members of organzied crime sindicates; in 1963 Bobby Kennedy had forced that figure up to 615 (there were 288 convictions).

In carrying out this policy, the Attorney-General was attacking a large segment of the power structure of the United States, since organized crime had links at every level, from congressmen down to mayors, from the head of the FBI down to local police chiefs.

Even the Kennedys themselves had become entangled with the mafia, through the various plots to assassinate Castro which they either authorized or tacitly approved, and through the President's liaison with Judith Campbell, a woman who was meeting JFK for secret assignations in the White House while also associating with Chicago mafia boss Sam Giancana. It is also believed that mafia control of voting in parts of Chicago may have been crucial in ensuring the narrow electoral victory that took Kennedy to the White House. Although it is not implied that the President himself took any part in organizing such corrupt

## Women in 1963

This was the year in which Betty Friedan published the book that is often credited as the foundation stone of the women's liberation movement: *The Feminine Mystique.* Friedan's target was the prevailing myth of woman as the ideal wife and mother — a myth that appeared to elevate women, while in reality relegating them firmly to the domestic sphere and a life of self-renunciation.

Friedan's outburst was much needed. There were no women in the inner councils of either the American or British governments of the day. Indeed, no woman exercised real political power anywhere in the world (although a few countries, like Britain, had a woman as formal head of state). The average wages of women in advanced industrial countries were about half those of men, and they were often paid far less than a man for doing exactly the same job.

They were also subjected to a whole range of rules that marked them as subject to male authority; in most places, for example, they could only obtain contraception, if at all, with their husband's express consent.

The media image of women still turned almost entirely on sex appeal. Although *Avengers'* star Honor Blackman presented a thoroughly active rôle model, her appeal obviously depended on glamour. Brigitte Bardot, currently starring in Jean-Luc Godard's *Le Mepris,* represented female liberation in her projection of woman as the possessor of desires, rather than their object — but was herself the quintessential object of male fantasy.

Beauty contests were uncontroversial and an ever-present source of journalistic copy. On 22 November it was announced that the newly-indepen-

**Slowly progressing up the political ladder in the early 1960s was Margaret Thatcher. She was appointed Joint Parliamentary Secretary to the Ministry of Pensions & National Insurance in October 1961. No one could have guessed that, within 15 years she would become leader of the Conservative Party and later the first woman British Prime Minister. *The Hulton-Deutsch Collection Ltd***

practices, he may well have been their unwitting beneficiary.

None of this deterred Bobby Kennedy from wielding his sword of righteousness. The most famous target of the attorney-general's zeal was the leader of the Teamsters Union, James Hoffa, who had close links with organized crime. Bobby Kennedy described the Teamsters as 'the most powerful institution in this country — aside from the United States government itself.' Under Hoffa's leadership it had become, he asserted, 'a conspiracy of evil.' The Justice Department had set up a unit dedicated exclusively to nailing Hoffa, and by November 1963 the Teamsters' leader was under indictment for jury tampering and misuse of union pension funds. He would eventually serve time for these offences, despite support from all his well placed friends in the political and legal system.

No comparable nexus of crime and corruption existed in Britain, but in the fashionable world of models, photographers, minor politicians, hairdressers and aspiring stars that formed the nucleus of what would, in two years' time, be termed Swinging London, the city's gang leaders, the Richardsons and the Krays, were familiar and accepted figures. The response to the Great Train Robbery, and especially popular revulsion at the heavy sentences imposed on its perpetrators, showed that a much wider British public felt no automatic revulsion at breaking the law, particularly if it was done with a minimum of violence and a great deal of efficiency. The Southampton University student union was to elect Bruce Reynolds, the chief organizer of the attack on the train, as a life member — and they were not out of step with public opinion.

In November 1963, soccer fans were enjoying one of the golden ages of the game in Britain. The top teams expected to knock in three or four goals in any home game; Tottenham had totalled 111 goals in 1962-63 without even winning the league. In 1963-64, four teams in the First Division were to score over 90 goals, Tottenham again top of the scoring with 97. In comparison, ten years later, playing the same number of games (42), no first division side scored more than 67 goals in the season.

Gates had fallen from the spectacular figures of the immediate postwar period,

dent state of Jamaica intended to celebrate the victory of Miss Jamaica, Carole Crawford, in the Miss World competition by putting her picture on the country's stamps. And the search for 'Miss *TV Times*' was underway, with the winner promised a prize of '£100 cash ... a TV test and a charm school course'. The position of women was changing, but not as the consequence of an ideological revolt. More women were going out to work, gaining financial independence, and using it. This was, for the moment, the driving force behind women's liberation.

***Top:*** **The newly crowned Miss World of 1963 was 20-year old Miss Jamaica, Carole Crawford. She is seen, in the company of Miss Germany (Susti Gruner), at an exhibition in Munich on 18 November 1963.** ***The Hulton-Deutsch Collection Ltd***

***Left:*** **By the early 1960s the pace of decolonisation was proceeding rapidly, as British possessions in Africa and the West Indies gained their independence. Carole Crawford, the Miss World of 1963, became the first living person, other than the reigning monarch, to feature on a Jamaican stamp.** ***The Hulton-Deutsch Collection Ltd***

## MARCELLO ON TRIAL

On the morning of 22 November 1963, Carlos Marcello, the mafia boss of Louisiana, was in a New Orleans courtroom awaiting the jury's verdict at the end of his trial on a charge of using false documents to obtain entry to the United States.

Marcello's criminal activities had made him one of the richest men in the United States, with a personal fortune in excess of $40 million. According to the House Select Committee on Assassinations, which later investigated Marcello in connection with the Kennedy assassination, the mafia leader enjoyed 'the corrupt collusion of public officials at every critical level, including police, sheriffs, judges, prosecutors, mayors, governors, licensing authorities, state legislators, and at least one member of congress.'

Since Marcello was officially a citizen of Guatemala (although he had been born in North Africa and spent most of his life in the United States), Bobby Kennedy had had him deported to his supposed homeland in 1961. Marcello's return to the United States had provided the pretext for the indictment.

Minutes before the Kennedy assassination, Marcello was acquitted predictably, since it was understandably difficult to obtain guilty verdicts from juries in cases involving the mafia. Some investigators of the assassination, including best-selling author John H. Davis, see Marcello as the most likely figure to have orchestrated a plot to kill the President. If so, the timing must have had an ironic aptness that would have appealed to the Cosa Nostra's well known sense of humour.

but were still impressive. The fact that 54,654 crowded into Old Trafford to see Manchester United play Liverpool that Saturday is perhaps not especially remarkable, but the attendance at Coventry for a match at the top of the Third Division was 23,901, more than the same club could attract for any game in the much-hyped Premier League of the 1990s. But then, the only football on television each week was 25 minutes of *Sports Special* (with Kenneth Wolstenholme) on a Saturday evening.

The footballer's maximum wage, which had restricted even the top stars to a salary little better than that of an average skilled worker, had been abolished the previous year after a tough campaign led by Jimmy Hill. This move had opened up new prospects for players who could achieve superstar status and the rewards that went with it. But it would also, over time, contribute in a change to the moral atmosphere of the game — and not for the better.

The schoolboys' heroes were then that now lost breed, the inside forwards: Johnny Haynes at Fulham (then a first division side), Eastham at Arsenal, and above all

**The New Zealand All-Blacks toured Britain during the 1963-64 season and, amongst many fixtures, played Oxford University at Iffley Road. *The Hulton-Deutsch Collection Ltd***

**The crowd at an Arsenal-Liverpool match at Highbury in 1963: it is interesting to note the lack of scarves and rossettes — as well as the complete lack of cover. *The Hulton-Deutsch Collection Ltd***

Jimmy Greaves at Tottenham, at this moment already scorer of 199 league goals and looking for the 200th which, in the way of these things, seemed to evade him from week to week. Matt Busby's Manchester United could field Bobby Charlton, Denis Law recently brought back from a disastrous spell in Italy, and a youngster who had just arrived at the club, George Best. Ron Greenwood's West Ham, destined to the win the FA Cup that season, was built around the modest but commanding presence of Bobby Moore. And at Stoke, hero-worship was focused on the elderly Stanley Matthews, already a figure from the mythical past, who had returned to the side the previous season like Lazarus raised from the dead and inspired them to promotion from the second division.

The league champions were Everton, who had won with a clear six point lead over second-placed Tottenham in 1962-63. The FA Cup holders were Manchester United, after a 3-1 win in the final against Leicester City (the second of Leicester's three cup final defeats in the 1960s). Top of the league on that Friday, however, were Sheffield United, with Liverpool, Blackburn and Tottenham in hot pursuit. Liverpool were to take over the top spot on the following day, and went on to win the league, for the first time since 1947. They would go on to win the championship 11 more times in the next 25 years, a period during which Everton also topped the league three times; the dominance of its football clubs was perhaps the most durable legacy for Liverpool from its annus

**Ted Dexter was the captain of the England cricket team. He is seen leading the players out for the First Test against the West Indies on 7 June 1963. *The Hulton-Deutsch Collection Ltd***

mirabilis. (It was also this year that the Liverpool fans adopted 'You'll Never Walk Alone' as their terrace song, from the Gerry and the Pacemakers' hit version.)

The great concern on the football pages of the newspapers on 22 November was mounting violence, both on the pitch and on the terraces. Everton had been forced by the Football Association to introduce England's first anti-hooligan barriers after objects had been thrown on to the pitch at two home games. But the barriers were only a few feet high and were restricted to the areas behind the goals. Their purpose was to keep fans at least six or seven yards from the goalkeepers — the usual targets for darts or other missiles. As the *Daily Mirror* admitted, the barriers were in practice futile, because they would not prevent objects being thrown into the goalmouth; it hardly needed a strong arm to throw a dart 20 feet. They were rather a gesture, an attempt to ward off criticism — typical of the football authorities' puny response to serious problems over the following years.

Nonetheless, the barriers were a sign of changing times. Desmond Hackett, writing in the *Daily Express*, perceived a decline in the traditional English superiority over foreigners. The barriers designed 'to keep ill-mannered, ill-tempered fans away from the pitch', had, according to Hackett, dealt a blow to 'the English worldwide reputation for sportsmanship'.

'I have always been proud of the unfettered playing-fields of England, when I looked upon the moats, caged-in pitches, military posts and regiments of police required to check the angers and aggressions of the foreign crowds... The passionate Italians are discouraged from violent physical protests by wired barricades rising 20 feet high... But for 100 years the tolerance and sportsmanship of the English spectators has required just the few quietly patrolling police, whose chief duties were to keep overexcited youngsters from running on to the pitch when their team has prospered.'

There was a long path ahead to the Heysel Stadium.

On the pitch, the *Daily Mirror* was concerned about dirty tricks that were going unpunished. Naïve readers were shown examples of the late tackle, the scissors tackle, going in over the top of the ball, and slicing the studs down an opponent's leg. The *Mirror* opined that the standard of conduct by professional players had never been so low. It was hoped, with undue optimism, that the use of cameras to check on foul play would help bring culprits to book during the 1966 World Cup, to be held, of course, in England. As it happened, this was to be one of the dirtiest of all World Cup competitions — the World Cup in which Pele was fouled and kicked into insignificance and the Argentinians behaved like 'animals'.

Unlike football, cricket had no problems of misbehaviour in the crowd or on the pitch — a lingering tradition of sportsmanship and fair play still held sway. But the game did face a financial crisis, which was at bottom a crisis of modernization. Cricket was a leisurely-paced game of 'gentlemen and players', a sport which still celebrated the virtues of amateurism and eccentricity, of the good loser rather than the single-minded winner. In the 1960s it threatened to become an anachronism.

Cricket lovers could bask in memories of one of the most dramatic test series ever played in England, the visit of the West Indies in the summer of 1963 which produced a tied test at Lords and outstanding performances from players such as Wes Hall, Tony Lock, Fred Trueman, Ted Dexter, Garfield Sobers, and Charlie Griffith. But cricket administrators knew that the game was near to bankruptcy and desperately needed to adapt to the new world of the 1960s, with its demand for instant excitement and its insistent commercial pressures.

In May 1963 they had first grasped the nettle and sacrificed the purity of the game to the twin gods of money and populism: the first one-day county game was played in England, between Lancashire and Leicestershire, in a knock-out competition sponsored by Gillette. The innovation was an outstanding popular and financial success. Some 25,000 spectators watched Sussex beat Worcestershire in the final of the tournament at Lords. From here the way lay open to one-day internationals, World Cups, Kerry Packer, and all the glitzy razzamatazz of the late 20th century game.

Tennis had not yet embarked on commercialization. The major competitions were amateur and players who went professional left fame and glory behind. Even here there were signs of change, how-

**The Austin Mini-Cooper S was the undoubted star of car rallies during the early 1960s, with a string of remarkable successes. One of these classic cars starts off at the beginning of the 1963 RAC rally.** ***Peter Roberts via Neill Bruce***

ever: Pierre Lacoste had just introduced the metal racket, a technological innovation that would transform the game in favour of power play. The sport was dominated by Australians — Rod Laver, Roy Emerson, and the unfortunate Fred Stolle who lost three Wimbledon finals in row, including the 1963 event which was won by Chuck McKinley of the United States. Australian star Margaret Smith (later Court) was the Wimbledon women's champion, having defeated the young Billie Jean Moffitt (later King), who was playing in the first of her nine Wimbledon singles finals.

Despite the retirement of Stirling Moss from grand prix racing, British drivers dominated the formula one world championship. Jim Clark, the Flying Scotsman, had clinched the title at Monza, Italy, in September, driving a Lotus 25 with a Coventry Climax engine. Second was Graham Hill, a reversal of the positions the previous year, when Hill had won the championship and Clark had been runner-up. In golf, on the other hand, the British had none of the dominance they would enjoy in the 1990s. This was the age of the American maestros Jack Nicklaus — winner of the US PGA and the Masters in 1963 — and Arnold Palmer, although a New Zealander, Bob Charles, had taken the British Open title held by Palmer for the previous two years.

Heavyweight boxing was also an exclusively American contest at the highest level — or, to be precise, exclusively *black* American. Floyd Patterson had established himself as a world champion of style and distinction, seemingly conforming to a liberal ideal of the 'responsible Negro.' In 1962, Patterson had been dislodged from the title by Sonny Liston, a shuffling giant with mobster connections — the sort of black man who scared and appalled white Americans. The contest between the two men paralleled, in a strange way, that between Martin Luther King Jr and Malcolm X — images of, from a white

# DAILY EXPRESS

No. 19,745 FRIDAY NOVEMBER 22 1963 Weather: Showery Price 3d.

## 1 a.m.: Dundee majority up

*SCOTTISH NATIONALIST HELPS TAKE VOTES FROM TORY*

# SOCIALIST IN BY 4,955

By CHARLES DOUGLAS-HOME

**THE Socialists won the Dundee West by-election early today with a majority up by more than 4,000. But it is not a great blow to the Tories —for a Scottish Nationalist intervened in the contest and took more than 3,000 votes.**

The result, announced after midnight:—

| | |
|---|---|
| Peter Doig (Soc.) | 22,449 |
| Dr. Robert Taylor (Tory) | 17,494 |
| Dr. James Lees (Scot. Nat.) | 3,285 |
| David Bowman (Com.) | 1,170 |
| Soc. majority | 4,955 |

In 1959 the late John Strachey (Socialist) had the small majority of 714.

The voting then was: Mr. Strachey 25,857, Dr. Taylor 25,143, Mr. Bowman 1,087.

In yesterday's contest, if the Scottish Nationalist had not stood, and all his supporters had voted Tory, the Socialist majority would still have been 1,670.

But from the percentage point of view the Socialists' victory is unimpressive. Their percentage increase in the poll was nine-tenths of one per cent.

WINNER DOIG 4,000 up

The Tories' share fell by 3.7 per cent.

Party leaders have no real cause either for extra rejoicing or deeper gloom from today's result.

Tory Party stalwarts maintain that the real turn of the tide mentioned by Sir Alec Douglas-Home after his Kinross by-election victory will not come until the St. Marylebone, Dumfries and Sudbury results come through next month.

### 'TRAGEDY'

MR. LEN WILLIAMS, general secretary of the Socialist Party, commented cheerfully early today:—

"The Prime Minister said that Luton was the end of a chapter and Kinross the beginning of a new one.

"Dundee is Page Two of the new chapter. For the Conservatives it must read like a Greek tragedy moving relentlessly towards its gloomy end.

"The increase in our majority is mighty satisfying."

Mr. Harold Wilson was not available for a comment.

MR. SELWYN LLOYD, awakened to hear the result in his London flat, commented: "The Labour Party think it is a Greek tragedy, do they?

"I think you must ask the Tory Party chairman what he thinks.

"I can't comment. It's none of my business."

### 'NEXT TIME'

MR. DOIG—a 52-year-old Dundee councillor — said: "The Prime Minister should regard this as the true voice of Scotland and declare a General Election."

DR. TAYLOR said: "When the next time comes, maybe it will be a different story."

The turn-out of voters, at 71 per cent, was 11 per cent down on the General Election.

Dr. Lees and Mr. Bowman lose their deposits.

## SUPREMO FOR SPACE DRIVE BY BRITAIN

By CHAPMAN PINCHER

EARL MOUNTBATTEN, the defence "Supremo," is to direct a big new drive to get Britain into the space business, speed the use of electronic brains and automation throughout industry, and boost exports.

He is to head a National Electronics Research Council charged with the job of stimulating Britain's electronic scientists and stemming the "brain-drain" to the U.S.

The earl, who is 63, is to be appointed to the job by Mr. Quintin Hogg, the Science Minister, because he has been the driving force behind its foundation. He has always been intensely interested in electronics.

*MOVE No. 2*

The National Electronics Research Council will consist of industrialists, scientists, and Government officials.

It is not yet known whether Earl Mountbatten, who is scheduled to stay as Chief of the Defence Staff for a further 18 months, will leave that post earlier or whether someone else will direct the new council until he is free.

In a further move to streamline the electronics industry, a conference of experts has been set up in line with "Neddy" — the National Economic Development Council.

The aim is to enable the industry to speak to the Government with one voice.

A meeting of the conference was held in London yesterday to discuss how the new council can speed Britain's efforts to get into the business of operating satellites for relaying telephone talks and TV.

### U2 pilot 'not in Cuba'

WASHINGTON, Thursday. — The pilot of a U2 spy plane which crashed off Florida after a mission over Cuba was still missing today.

There is speculation here that he may have baled out over Cuba, but Defence Department officials do not put much weight on the possibility. Mechanical failure is said to have caused the crash.

### Tree hits roof

### Ship aground

### Rhino whip case meeting today

### Six flee blast

### New Ford strike threat

NEW TROUBLE loomed at Fords Dagenham plant last night when 1,200 press shop workers gave a fortnight's notice of strike because about 300 colleagues are not paying union subscriptions.

A check on union cards showed many men had not paid for 13 weeks and some for up to a year. Several unions are involved. The paid-up members say they are working

## LOOK OUT!

### THE GILES FAMILY HEADS NORTH...

GILES is on the move—and that's when the fun starts.

The irrepressible Express cartoonist (with Grandma and the children in tow, of course) is in the North . . . land of opportunity, as ex-Lord Hailsham calls it.

And what an opportunity for the Giles family to ring the bell! Look out for their adventures in the North. And now see the announcement by Giles jun. on **Page 12 TODAY.**

**WATCH THE EXPRESS NEXT WEEK**

### Journey to the Land of Long Life

**LEONARD MOSLEY** has journeyed to a fantastic Shangri La where the people live so long and look so young.

They look like 20-year-olds at 70. They can hear each other whisper from a distance of a quarter of a mile. They never die of heart failure. They never grow stooped. They die only when their bodies wear out, and that is when they are very, very old.

What is their secret? What can we learn from them?

Watch the Express NEXT WEEK

## *STEWART TOP IN 'SHADOW' POLL*

By CHARLES DOUGLAS-HOME

MR. MICHAEL STEWART, Opposition spokesman on housing, topped the poll in the Shadow Cabinet ballot, results of which were announced to a meeting of Socialist M.P.s last night.

Mr. Stewart, M.P. for Fulham, collected 184 votes, nine more than the next man, Shadow Chancellor Mr. James Callaghan.

Last year Mr. Callaghan topped the poll and Mr. Stewart was in eighth place.

His popularity can be put down to Socialist backbenchers' high regard for his crisp speeches on housing since Rachmanism blew up into a party issue.

*NOTED*

Backbenchers particularly noted Mr. Stewart's speech at the Socialist Party Conference and on the housing amendment to the Local Address on Monday.

There are no new members of the Shadow Cabinet. It consists, in the following order, of Mr. Stewart, Mr. Callaghan, Mr. Douglas Houghton, Sir Frank Soskice, Mr. Patrick Gordon Walker, Mr. Tom Fraser, Mr. Denis Mr. Fred Lee, Mr. Fred Willey, Mr. Douglas Jay, and Mr. G. R. Mitchison.

Mr. Richard Crossman topped the list of candidates who were not elected.

TORY backbenchers last night took revenge on Mr. Charles Curran, M.P. for Uxbridge, for the lighthearted mauling he gave the Prime Minister on his first appearance in the Commons last week.

Mr. Curran was not re-elected to the executive committee of the 1922 Committee, consisting of all Tory backbenchers.

### Driver kidnapped Yard told

## Schoolboy pulls K's leg in outer space

By JOHN KING

THAT English ploughman who wanted to cut a furrow to the stars in a Russian spaceship brushed back his semi-Beatle cut, took a long swig of pop, and said yesterday: "The joke on Mr. Krushchev has gone too far.

"Why" went on 17-year-old Ashley Adams, "I wouldn't live in Russia if they paid me.

"As for being a cosmonaut, that's far too much of an up-and-down life."

ASHLEY ADAMS Joke over

*Yarn-spinner*

Ashley prefers yarn-spinning. He works as a laboratory assistant in a Stroud, Gloucestershire nylon factory and has never touched a plough in his life.

And the nearest he has ever got to a spacecraft is the Flying Machine, a completely earth-bound pub at Brockworth.

Then how comes it a report was sent round the world from Moscow that he had asked to be trained as a Soviet spaceman because in Russia a ploughman had the same chance of being a cosmonaut as anybody else?

"That," explained Ashley after another swig of pop "was my last prank as a schoolboy—nearly a year ago.

"I'd wanted to train as a nuclear scientist at Harwell, but was turned down.

*Just a bet*

"Then my fifth form pals at Marling School, Stroud, bet me some tuck that I dare not write for a spaceman's job in Russia.

"I remembered Krushchev was brought up in a small town so I wrote saying I was a ploughman interested in technical advances in agriculture."

He addressed the letter to Mr. Krushchev and sent it to the Russian Embassy in London. On it went to Moscow in the diplomatic bag — to be published months later in a Russian newspaper.

### Summit call

NEW YORK, Thursday.—Russia today proposed that next year's session of the United Nations General Assembly should be held at Heads-of-State level.

**POCKET CARTOON** by OSBERT LANCASTER

*"Tell me, officer, has there been much mental illness in your division recently?"*

## *GETAWAY! WIFE PUTS LUNCH IN OVEN AND FLIES OFF*

Express Staff Reporter

SHE waved goodbye to her 12-year-old daughter and said: "Don't be late home." Then Mrs. Betty Larking dusted the house as usual, cooked the lunch, laid the table—and vanished.

Now her husband George has discovered that while he and his two children were eating the meal she had prepared, 45-year-old Mrs. Larking was flying to a new life in America.

So secret had she kept her plans that not a relative knew where she had gone. Her daughter Trudy and 18-year-old son Anthony were completely in the dark.

### Remembered

At first, Mr Larking thought his wife might be with friends.

Then, after reporting her to the police as missing, he remembered her writing to an employment agency.

He called there and learned the staggering truth—for three months Mrs. Larking had been making elaborate plans to leave England.

Without anybody knowing she went to London to be interviewed by a New York family who wanted a home help. She obtained an air ticket, took out a passport—and kept them secret until her getaway 12 days ago.

### 'So happy'

Mr Larking said last night at his home in Wexham-court, Slough: "I couldn't be more flabbergasted. I can honestly say we've had 20 happy years together."

Mrs. Ruby Parker, principal of the employment agency, said: "If we had known Mrs. Larking was doing all this secretly we would not have considered her."

### Britain denies it

WASHINGTON, Thursday — A British Embassy spokesman in Washington tonight denied a report that Britain has agreed to take part in the experimental crewing of a test ship to see if a Nato mixed - manned Polaris nuclear force is technically feasible.

### Boy hunt widens

Interpol yesterday joined the hunt for Christopher Pearce, 16-year-old son of Twickenham councillor Mr. Kenneth Pearce who left home 18 days ago after receiving a letter from a West Berlin pen friend.

### TV romance

Judith Chalmers, 28-year-old TV announcer, is marrying B.B.C. producer Neil Durden-Smith, aged 30, in the New Year. Miss Chalmers's first marriage was dissolved.

### Old lamps for new

Old oil lamps were brought into use again in many village homes last night when a power failure blacked out a large area of West Suffolk, centred around Clare.

## *JUST FANCY THAT*

A CASE against two men accused of an attack in an Indian restaurant was held up for two hours yesterday at Banbury, Oxfordshire, while police tried to find a Koran and a Hindu holy book for two Indian witnesses. Eventually the Hindu gave evidence without taking an oath, and the Moslem was not called—although police brought a Koran

## BOAC chief: £15,000

**PAY RATE GOES UP FOR A DOUBLE JOB**

Express Staff Reporter

THE new "overlord" of British Overseas Airways, 47-year-old merchant banker Sir Giles Guthrie, is to get £15,000 a year plus £1,000 expenses. And he will be sacrificing about £5,000 by taking on the job.

This was revealed last night by Mr. Julian Amery, the Aviation Minister.

The salary of B.O.A.C.'s outgoing chief, Sir Matthew Slattery, is £8,500.

*THE JOB*

But Sir Giles, pilot and part-time member of the B.E.A. board, will be doing a dual job as chairman and managing director.

Express Political Correspondent writes: The Government will start to write off B.O.A.C.'s £80,000,000 deficit when Sir Guthrie produces his plan to make the airline financially sound. That was the firm impression given to Tory M.P.s by Mr. Amery at a private meeting in the Commons last night.

White-paper: Page 4
New boss: Page 12

### Wall-street drops

NEW YORK, Thursday.—A wave of selling hit Wall-street today when £1,700 million was wiped off share values. The tumble in prices was the biggest so far this year.

Altogether 5,676,000 shares were traded. One leading stock fell by just under £13 each. The share index dropped 9.41 points to 722.65.

### No escape

The Metropolitan Police will NOT be told by the Home Secretary to stop "protecting" the Beatles from their admirers, Mr. Christopher Woodhouse, Home Office Under-Secretary said in a Commons reply yesterday: "It is the duty of the police to take any necessary steps to prevent disorder."

### Knife men chased

More than 20 people chased two bandits armed with knives who had grabbed £40 from a watchmaker's shop in South Molton-street, Mayfair, last night.

**RADIO, TV Page 22**

FLEet-street 8000



**In Britain, on 22 November 1963, the news was dominated by the result of the Dundee West by-election, which the Labour candidate, Peter Doig, won with an increased majority. There was no Liberal candidate — how times change. Although the tenor of the *Daily Express*'s article is generally favourable to the Conservatives, the political tide was turning against Prime Minister Alec Douglas-Home, who went on to lose the 1964 General Election.**

liberal point of view, the acceptable and unacceptable faces of black America. In the wings, however, an Olympic champion called Cassius Clay was waiting his turn. In February 1964 he would defeat Liston in a contest of brain against brawn, and Muhammad Ali would prove far more challenging to white Americans than either of the previous champions in those politicised times.

The headline news in Britain on 22 November was another disastrous by-election defeat for the Conservative government. In the Dundee West constituency, Labour had increased its majority from 714 at the previous general election to 4,955, 'proof positive', as the *Daily Express* wrote, 'that the tide is still running hard against the government'. A young Neil Kinnock was attending that evening a debate at the Cardiff Students' Union on the motion: 'This house believes that the end of conservatism is nigh.' After almost 13 years of continuous Tory rule, and four years after an election that had left political commentators braying that Labour would never form a government again, the triumph of the opposition seemed almost a certainty.

British politics was still reeling from the impact of the Profumo scandal. On 22 March 1963, the Minister for War (we were not yet so mealey-mouthed as to have a Minister for Defence) John Profumo had been obliged to respond to allegations about his relations with a certain Christine Keeler. The minister informed the House of Commons that: 'There was no impropriety whatsoever in my acquaintanceship with Miss Keeler.' This was a straight lie, and was soon conclusively demonstrated to be such.

Profumo had met Keeler, then 19 years old, by Lord Astor's poolside in 1961. She was a nude dancer who had been introduced into aristocratic company by her protector, Stephen Ward, a society osteopath and amateur artist. Keeler was a great success in the sexually sophisticated world of vice that Ward frequented, taking part in the sex-club orgies and wife-swapping sessions with which that section of the upper class entertained itself. As well as Profumo, her lovers included the distasteful Peter Rachman, who had got rich through the crudest exploitation of private tenants in his empire of slums, and, unfortunately for Profumo, the quite personable, fun-loving naval attaché at the Soviet Embassy, Eugene Ivanvov.

The inside story of the espionage angle of the Profumo affair is still not fully clear. MI5 had definitely asked Ward to bring Keeler and Ivanov together, presumably in an attempt to entrap the Russian, who would then be blackmailed into working for the British. But whether Profumo simply blundered innocently onto this scene, or was himself the target of a Soviet operation through Ivanov, is not known. Ivanov certainly asked Keeler to pass on to him secrets picked up from Profumo's pillow talk, and some of this information, about nuclear weapons in West Germany, may have had a certain value.

In any event, the fact that the Minister for War had been sharing a girlfriend with the Soviet naval attaché was a sufficient scandal. By 5 June the evidence against Profumo was overwhelming; he was forced to admit his misdeeds and resign from the government. As evidence of an intelligence disaster, these revelations were damaging to the government. It completed a deeply embarassing series of spy scandals, from the uncovering of George Blake as a long-term Soviet agent in the British intelligence service in 1961; the Vassall case in 1962, in which an admiralty clerk, blackmailed by the KGB for his homosexuality, was shown to have been passing secrets to the Soviets for years; and the defection of Kim Philby to the Soviet Union in January 1963, which had finally revealed the extraordinary extent of Soviet penetration of the British secret service.

Far more striking from the public's point of view, however, were the sexual revelations that tumbled across the pages of the cheaper Sunday papers, shadowed by a wealth of unpublished rumours that were even more salacious and damning in their detail of perversion ana

No. 19,600

DAILY EXPRESS

THURSDAY JUNE 6 1963

1 a.m. forecast: Sunny; thundery

Price 3d.

PROFUMO QUITS: I LIED

He gives up War Minister's job and seat in House of Commons

His denial of impropriety with Christine Keeler was untrue... 'I misled you,' he tells Premier

Express Political Correspondent IAN AITKEN

MR. JOHN PROFUMO resigned from the Government last night, and will quit Parliament too—because, he admitted, he lied to the Prime Minister and the House of Commons when he said there was "no impropriety" in his relationship with model girl Christine Keeler.

The 48-year-old War Minister left his London home with his wife, former actress Valerie Hobson, a few hours before the announcement that shattered Westminster.

In a letter to Mr. Macmillan, Mr. Profumo said that "by this deception I have been guilty of a grave misdemeanour."

He also mentioned rumours circulated three months ago about "the disappearance of a 'witness'" and "some possible breach of security."

NO NAMES

Mr. Profumo gave no names, but was apparently referring to two people:—

Christine Keeler, 21, who vanished last March when due to appear as a witness at a trial of her former friend, Jamaican John Edgecombe.

Eugene Ivanov, Russian assistant naval attaché in London and friend of Miss Keeler, who was recalled to Moscow last December.

Last night Miss Keeler was believed to be staying at a flat in Jubilee-place, Chelsea.

There, a short, dark man with an American accent said: "I am acting as business manager for Miss Keeler but at the moment there is nothing either of us can say."

The telephone in the flat kept ringing. "I am extremely busy," the man said. "I have a lot of business to transact."

Yesterday morning Mr. and Mrs. Profumo drove off from their white, two-storey Nash house in Chester-terrace, Regent's Park, in their 3.8 Jaguar.

SURPRISE

Mr. Stanley Brisco, Mr. Profumo's butler for 15 years, stood at the black door of the house later and said: "I must say I was a bit surprised at their going away.

"They only got back from holiday at the beginning of the week.

Dear P.M.

MR. PROFUMO, from Chester-terrace, Regent's Park, wrote to Mr. Macmillan:—

Dear Prime Minister,

You will recollect that on March 22, following certain allegations made in Parliament, I made a personal statement.

At that time rumour had charged me with assisting in the disappearance of a witness and with being involved in some possible breach of security.

So serious were these charges that I allowed myself to think that my personal association with that witness, which had also been the subject of rumour, was by comparison of minor importance only.

In my statement I said that there had been no impropriety in this association. To my very deep regret I have to admit that this was not true and that I misled you and my colleagues, and the House.

'My wife was misled'

I ask you to understand that I did this to protect, as I thought, my wife and family, who were equally misled, as were my professional advisers.

I have come to realise that, by this deception, I have been guilty of a grave misdemeanour, and despite the fact that there is no truth whatever in the other charges, I cannot remain a member of your Administration, nor of the House of Commons.

I cannot tell you of my deep remorse for the embarrassment I have caused to you, to my colleagues in the Government, to my constituents, and to the party which I have served for the past 25 years.

Yours sincerely, JACK PROFUMO.

Dear Profumo

MR. MACMILLAN replied from Connel, Argyll, where he is on holiday:—

Dear Profumo,

The contents of your letter of June 4 have been communicated to me, and I have heard them with deep regret. This is a great tragedy for you, your family, and your friends.

Nevertheless I am sure you will understand that, in the circumstances, I have no alternative but to advise the Queen to accept your resignation.

Yours very sincerely,
HAROLD MACMILLAN.

Mr. Profumo and wife, former actress Valerie Hobson

BACK-BENCH LABOUR MPs AIM FOR STORM

By ARTHUR BUTLER

POCKET CARTOON by OSBERT LANCASTER

'Nazi' shouts greet General

South-East cuts jobless total

20 killed in riots

Ricketts fails to convince Britain

Earl Attlee opposes

Crowds stampede at St. Peter's

New federation

England win 8—1

4 a.m. LATEST

FLEet-street 8000

FERRARI TALKS WITH B.M.C.

By BASIL CARDEW



*Above left:* Earlier in the year, British politics had been rocked by the Profumo scandal. John Profumo, the War Minister, who had made a statement to the House of Commons denying any impropriety in his relationship with Christine Keeler, pictured right, was forced to resign when it appeared that he had been lying.

*Left:* One of the leading players in the Profumo Scandal, Stephen Ward, committed suicide at the height of the affair. Inevitably, there was great interest in his lifestyle — including his amateur painting. A collection of his pictures was displayed for a time at a south London pub. *The Hulton-Deutsch Collection Ltd*

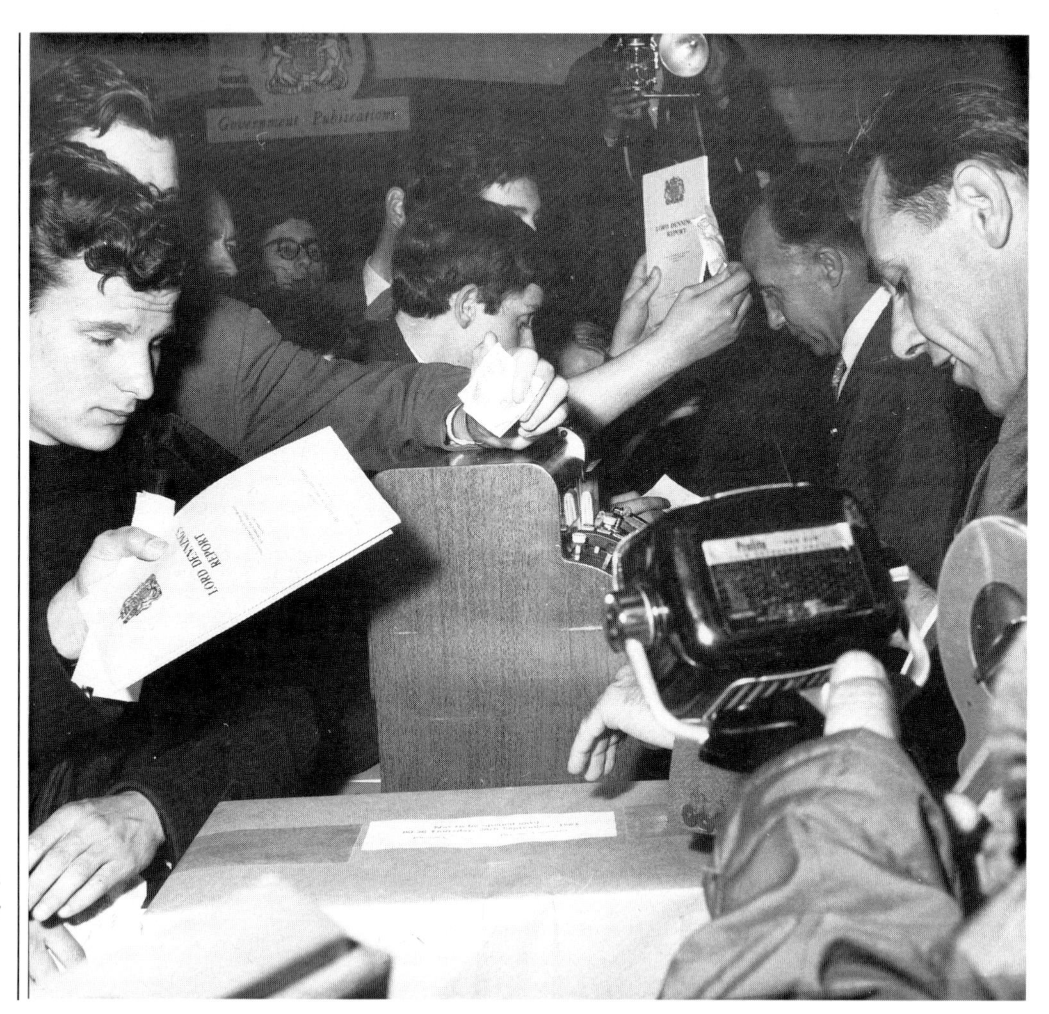


*Right:* **Lord Denning was appointed to investigate the security implications of the Profumo Affair and, when issued in late September 1963, there was a great rush to obtain copies. Inevitably, satirists got in on the act; the popular musical duo of Michael Flanders and Donald Swann even claiming, at one stage, to be investigating Denning 'for security, you know'.** ***The Hulton-Deutsch Collection Ltd***

*Below:* **The early 1960s witnessed a rush amongst peers to renounce their titles and return to the House of Commons. First to make the attempt to renounce his title formally was Anthony Wedgwood Benn, who had become the second Viscount Stansgate on the death of his father. As a result of Benn's campaign, an act was passed to allow peers to renounce titles, thus paving the way for Alec Douglas-Home to return to the Commons as Prime Minister after the resignation of Harold MacMillan in 1963.** ***The Hulton-Deutsch Collection Ltd***

prostitution. (On 22 November, the *Daily Mirror* was reprimanded by the Press Council for publishing a front page story which had purported to repudiate 'the foul rumour' that Prince Philip was involved in the scandal. Of course, by repudiating the rumour so prominently, they simply spread it further.) A Sunday paper allegedly paid Christine Keeler £23,000 for her story (more than 20 times the annual average wage) and it was well worth the newspaper's money. A picture taken by the fashionable photographer Lewis Morley, showing Keeler naked astride an ultra-modern Arne Jacobsen chair, became one of the period's most memorable icons.

The resignation of Profumo, followed by Ward's trial on a trumped-up charge of pimping and his subsequent suicide, eventually laid the case to rest. On 22 November Christine Keeler was awaiting the outcome of a charge of perjury and conspiracy to pervert the course of justice, which had resulted from her testimony during the trial of an ex-boyfriend, West Indian jazz singer Lucky Gordon, for an assault upon her the previous year. On 6 December Keeler was sentenced to nine months in prison. She later described her time in Holloway as 'a bit of peace' after the traumas of the previous year.

The effect of the Profumo affair on British politics was to confirm the popular impression of a corrupt and decadent establishment clinging on to power without competence, patriotism or morality. It led indirectly to the resignation of Prime Minister Harold Macmillan, who was in ill health and had seemed increasingly out of touch through the crisis. The selection of a successor was hopelessly botched, however. With no formal election procedure to hamper them, the Conservative leadership indulged in an orgy of bickering and back-stabbing, resulting in the selection of a mild compromise candidate, Lord Home, rather than the younger, more popular 'Rab' Butler.

Home was an astonishing choice, a soft-spoken aristocrat as distant from the modern world as any politician could be. He was able to renounce his peerage — a right recently fought for and won by Anthony Wedgewood Benn — and sit in the House of Commons, but nothing could make him connect with the images of youth and modernity that were the spirit of the times.

**At the time of Kennedy's assassination, campaigning was taking place in another crucial by-election — that of the St Marylebone constituency in London — when Quentin Hogg, who had also renounced his title of Lord Hailsham, sought to return to the Commons. The actual ballot took place on 5 December. *The Hulton-Deutsch Collection Ltd***

On 22 November, Home had been prime minister for just over one month. Two of Macmillan's ministers, Enoch Powell and Ian Macleod, had refused to serve under him. His cabinet included Reginald Maudling as Chancellor of the Exchequer, Henry Brooke as a much reviled Home Secretary, and Edward Heath as Secretary of State for Industry, Trade and Regional Development. Opposing this government was a shadow cabinet led by Harold Wilson, who had taken over the leadership of the opposition after the death of Hugh Gaitskell the previous January. Wilson was

**Watched by Russian premier Khruschev, Cuban leader Fidel Castro takes a photo in Moscow during his first visit to the Soviet Union.**
***The Hulton-Deutsch Collection Ltd***

everything that Home was not — brash, clever, classless, young, thoroughly modern, and politically effective. According to Wilson, the 'white heat' of a technological revolution was going to transform Britain and return it to a leading place among the nations. State planning would encourage growth and progressive taxation of the rich would create a more egalitarian society. With such ideas, Labour held the intellectual high ground. It seemed certain they would be returned to government the following year, as indeed they were.

On 22 November 1963, the focus of world politics was on the confrontation between the two superpowers, the United States and the Soviet Union. At the head of the Soviet state was Nikita Khrushchev, a flamboyant showman with a touch of the erratic gambler to his nature that worried his own apparatchiks. Facing him was, of course, J. F. Kennedy, himself an aggressive man of action willing to take risks to get what he wanted. These two adventurers had brought the world to the brink of nuclear war in the Cuban Missile Crisis of 1962, but since war had been averted both, somewhat irrationally, enjoyed wide popular esteem.

East and West faced one another as mirror images, the Nato alliance on one side, the Warsaw Pact on the other, bandying propaganda and endlessly increasing their nuclear weaponry to a point of massive overkill. If anything, the initiative in the world contest between capitalism and communism lay with the Soviet camp. Khrushchev had threatened to 'bury capitalism' and his bumptious optimism was boosted by the Soviet lead in the space race. 'We give capitalism another seven years,' he told American journalists in November 1963, 'Then we will be first. It is as inevitable as the sunrise.'

A Europe divided between East and West, communism and capitalism, was an accepted state of affairs that no one any longer expected to change. Its symbol was Berlin, divided since August 1961 by a heavily guarded wall. The mayor of capitalist West Berlin, Willy Brandt, was a hero of Western resistance to the advance of communism, but he was also prepared to work with the communist East, accepting the inevitability of the status quo that Soviet military might imposed. The Soviets, for their part, secretly accepted that West Berlin, and Western Europe, would remain under the control of the American-led Nato; these were the rules imposed by nuclear stalemate.

The East-West divide was not the only split in Europe, however. Salazar's Portugal and, to a much greater extent, Franco's Spain stood to one side as remnants of the era of fascist dictatorship. They were poor and backward countries with economies and political systems out of step with West

European liberal democracy. Yugoslavia, ruled by the wartime resistance leader Marshal Tito, ploughed its own furrow as an independent communist state, authoritarian rule effectively holding in check the nationalist aspirations of the different elements of the Yugoslav population.

At the heart of Western Europe, France, West Germany, Italy, Belgium, the Netherlands and Luxembourg had formed the Common Market. Britain wanted to join this Europe of 'the Six' and had entered into lengthy negotiations, conducted by an aspiring Conservative politician, Edward Heath. But France was led by the ultra-nationalist General Charles de Gaulle, whose greatest ambition was to assert his country's independence of the United States. He had ordered American nuclear bombers off his territory in 1960 and was developing an independent French nuclear armoury. Britain, on the other hand, had agreed to be supplied with Polaris missiles by the United States. Convinced that the British were lap-dogs of the Americans, he vetoed their entry into the Common Market in January 1963.

Both Britain and France had accepted that the days of empire were over. Even Algeria, which France had almost destroyed herself trying to hold, had at last been relinquished to independence (making the streets of Paris safe from terrorist outrages after a nightmare period of bombings and shootings). With virtually every month that passed a new country joined the burgeoning ranks of the United Nations. 'Coloured' heads of state, almost unknown five years earlier, were now commonplace. On 22 November, Kenya was preparing for independence under Jomo Kenyatta, once denounced as a terrorist. In Ghana, Kwame Nkrumah ruled, a leader of great international prestige but increasingly resented by his own people. The mood in Africa was still

**Throughout black Africa the tide of independence was running strong as Britain, France and Belgium retreated from empire. The 'Winds of Change' that MacMillan had foreseen brought great changes to the whole African continent. Exactly one week before Kennedy's death, on 15 November 1963, the Mayor of Berlin (and future German Chancellor) Willy Brandt met Jomo Kenyatta, who was soon to become President of independent Kenya.** ***The Hulton-Deutsch Collection Ltd***

**In South Africa, the forces of Apartheid ensured that repressive policies towards the country's black majority continued. The African National Congress was under attack with its leaders, such as Nelson Mandela (seen here before his imprisonment for life in June 1964), under arrest. *The Hulton-Deutsch Collection Ltd***

one of post-colonial optimism, but already military regimes were replacing civilian ones with depressing frequency, and one newly independent state, the Congo (now Zaïre), had been torn apart by civil war, outside military intervention, and the breakdown of order.

Continuing resistance to black majority rule in sub-Saharan Africa was restricted to the Portuguese colonies of Guinea-Bissau, Angola and Mozambique, where there were already stirrings of guerrilla warfare; the British colony of Southern Rhodesia, where white settlers opposed plans to grant independence under majority rule; and South Africa, with its colony, Namibia. The South African government was set on strengthening its policy of apartheid and hardening white minority rule. Nelson Mandela, the only black South African leader of real stature, had been arrested and was awaiting trial.

The independent non-European states, constituting what was now known as the Third World, were a battleground for the communist and capitalist ideologies. Many of them found the communist model more attractive, although the Americans and Europeans had more money and better equipment to offer. Communism had, after all, been an ideology of resistance to colonialism, and it was viewed as an economic success in the Soviet Union and China. Indeed, China was often favourably compared to India, which had followed a mitigated capitalist road to development and was widely regarded as falling headlong into a mire of poverty and overpopulation.

Ruled by the formidable Mao Tse-tung, China presented itself as a model for Third World peasant countries to follow. Mao had split with the Soviet Union over ideology — Khrushchev's relative liberalism was unacceptable to Peking's dedicated revolutionaries and because the Russians were reluctant to help him develop nuclear weapons. This fissure in the communist world, until recently regarded as a monolithic bloc, was much exercising political commentators in the West in 1963. China was entirely boycotted by the United States — there was no trade between the two countries, and any American citizen visiting China was liable to severe consequences on return to the United States — but the potential for playing off the Chinese against the Soviets was already apparent. While Mao continued to denounce 'imperialism' with such vehemence and encourage world revolution, however, China remained third on Washington's list of international enemies.

Enemy number one on that list was the Soviet Union, despite the détènte that had followed the resolution of the Cuban missile crisis. Number two was Cuba itself. The existence of a communist state in America's own backyard was an unbearable irritation, not soothed by the repressed knowledge that it was probably American hostility that had driven Cuba's revolutionary leader, Fidel Castro, into the arms of Moscow.

Castro had proved a true survivor. After an American economic embargo that wrecked the Cuban economy, an American-backed invasion by Cuban exiles (the Bay of Pigs, 1961), the threat of a direct American military onslaught (the Cuban Missile Crisis,

1962), and numerous plots against his life by the CIA and the mafia (not known to the public until the 1970s, but at least partially known to Castro himself), he still ruled his country in a truly original and, at the time, truly popular style, with his Argentinian lieutenant Che Guevara at his side. President Kennedy's handling of the Cuban issue — his failure to back the Bay of Pigs invasion to the hilt and his refusal to launch a military strike against the country during the Missile Crisis — had earned him many enemies, not only among right-wing Cuban exiles, but also in his own intelligence community and among the top US military staff.

In general, Kennedy's high world standing was more a matter of image than substance. His tour of Europe in the summer of 1963 had been a triumphal progress, a parade of youth and glamour to which the First Lady contributed as much as the President (or more: Kennedy self-

## THAT WAS THE WEEK THAT WAS ADDRESSES LORD HOME

On 19 October, the BBC's Saturday night satire programme *That Was The Week That Was* responded to the elevation of the 14th Earl of Home to the premiership with the following address, delivered by the show's presenter, David Frost:

'My Lord: when I say that your acceptance of the Queen's commission to form an administration has proved, and will prove, an unmitigated catastrophe for the Conservative Party, for the Constitution, for the Nation, and for yourself, it must not be thought that I bear you any personal ill-will... You are the dupe and unwitting tool of a conspiracy — the conspiracy of a tiny band of desperate men who have seen in you their last slippery chance of keeping the levers of power within their privileged circle. For the sake of that prize, which can at best be transitory, those men are prepared to dash all the hopes of the Party they profess to serve: or rather the two nations which by their actions they seek to perpetuate... And so there is the choice for the electorate; on the one hand Lord Home — and on the other hand Mr Harold Wilson. Dull Alec versus Smart Alec.'

**By the early 1960s the Communist world was split into two power blocks headed by the Soviet Union and China. The Chinese Communist leader, Mao Tse-Tung, celebrated his 60th birthday in 1963. It was not to be long before he launched his great purge of the Chinese state — the Cultural Revolution — which was to mark the final years of his rule. *The Hulton-Deutsch Collection Ltd***

## An Irish joke

On 22 November 1963, British Prime Minister Sir Alec Douglas Home entertained the Prime Minister of Northern Ireland, Captain Terence O'Neill, for a cosy lunch at 10 Downing Street.

The party that Home led was then the Conservative and Unionist Party, fully committed to upholding the Union between Britain and Northern Ireland and Protestant rule in that province. The government at Stormont, which had extensive powers over the internal affairs of Northern Ireland, treated the Catholic element of the population as second-class citizens in every respect — housing, employment, education, voting rights, civil liberties.

Despite this injustice and an unemployment rate three to four times the British average, there was no substantial popular unrest in Northern Ireland. The division of Ireland was contested by the Irish Republican Army (IRA), but its efforts at an armed struggle were ineffectual. A campaign of raids on border posts had been called off in 1962 after some farcical failures. There had been no IRA terrorist outrages in mainland Britain since before World War 2, and the organization was generally regarded by the English as an Irish joke.

**The day before Kennedy's assassination Sir Alec Douglas-Home, now safely re-elected to the Commons, met Capt Terence O'Neill, the Prime Minister of Northern Ireland, at 10 Downing Street.** ***The Hulton-Deutsch Collection Ltd***

mockingly introduced himself as 'the man who accompanied Jacqueline Kennedy to Paris'). Khrushchev's popularity in the West was equally based on his ebullient personality, rather than his policies. *Newsweek* magazine, for example, referred to Khrushchev as 'Russia's number one stand-up comedian', and a popular article on the Soviet premier in the *TV Times,* written by David Ennals, focussed on his 'astonishing physical vitality... dynamic, unpredictable, excitable — a jack-in-the-box of a man.'

Both Khrushchev and Kennedy had much more trouble convincing their domestic audiences, both the people and the politicians, of their worth. Khrushchev faced a crisis in agriculture, declining industrial production, and criticism of an adventurous foreign policy that had led to retreat over Cuba and a split with China. His mild liberalization of the Soviet Union had frightened the bureaucrats without satisfying the intellectuals. Although the world did not know it, his hold on power was already tenuous.

Kennedy was also in domestic trouble. Americans were susceptible to the administration's media charisma. Jacqueline's stylish redecoration of the White House; the charm of the Kennedy children, always in the limelight, especially John who would be three years old on November 25; and the President himself representing, as Norman Mailer wrote, 'America's romantic dream of itself'. But he had many bitter opponents, not only Republicans such as the presidential candidate he had defeated, Richard Nixon, and the candidate he was likely to face in the next presidential election, the hawkish Senator Barry Goldwater, but also Democrats from the South, such as Governor George C. Wallace of Alabama, whose hostility to racial integration overrode any other political allegiances.

Kennedy had been slow to introduce civil rights legislation to counter the effects of American racism because he knew it would cost him votes. Prejudice against blacks was widespread in the United States, as elsewhere in the world. (Immigration into Britain was running at around 90,000 a year, and the British newspapers on 22 November reported calls by Tory MPs to impose severe restrictions on new arrivals — because, of course, they were not white). The mounting civil rights campaign led by Martin Luther King Jr. had, however, forced the president's hand.

The year had been a traumatic but triumphant one for the black struggle. The excesses of white racism in the face of non-violent protest had shamed America and shocked world opinion. In May, in Birmingham, Alabama, black women and children engaged in a peaceful demonstration had been attacked with dogs, fire hoses and clubs. On 11 June, Medgar Evers, a prominent Mississippi black activist, was murdered, triggering widespread demonstrations. And four black children were killed when racists bombed a Birmingham church. Fired by the indignation these events provoked, 200,000 people sympathetic to the cause of civil rights gathered at the Lincoln Memorial in Washington on 28 August, to hear King deliver his immortal 'I have a dream' speech. Present were a host of liberal-minded stars, including Marlon Brando, Burt Lancaster, Judy Garland, Bob Dylan and Joan Baez, Harry Belafonte, the folk group Peter, Paul and Mary, and Mahalia Jackson singing 'We Shall Overcome'.

This event, which epitomised the pious, sober, courageous tone of protest in the early 1960s, was far from winning universal approval, however. Not only white racists opposed it. Malcolm X, then the most famous spokesman for the Black Muslim movement, the Nation of Islam, viewed 'that circus' with cynical contempt. More representative of feeling in the ghettos of the Northern cities than the Southern

***Right:*** **The Governor of Alabama, George Wallace, was one of the most well-known opponents of the civil rights movement in the USA. Later himself to be a victim of an assassination attempt, Wallace was to campaign for the presidency from a wheelchair. *The Hulton-Deutsch Collection Ltd***

***Right:*** **1963 was marked by racial tension throughout the southern states of the USA. In Birmingham, Alabama, members of the National States Rights Party hung an effigy of civil rights leader Martin Luther King Jr outside the party's headquarters as a protest against the black demonstrations held in the city.** ***The Hulton-Deutsch Collection Ltd***

Martin Luther King, Malcolm X opposed the tactic of non-violence and the goal of integration with white society. King's movement wanted blacks to be accepted as equals, to be able to vote and hold public office — both impossible through much of the South — and to mix with whites in all public places and social circumstances. Malcolm X and other separatists wanted to emphasise the specific qualities that blacks possessed, and to denounce white society rather than join it.

Also opposed to King was the head of the FBI, J. Edgar Hoover. On 21 October 1963 Bobby Kennedy authorized Hoover to tap King's telephone, supposedly to establish whether some members of the SCLC (Southern Christian Leadership Conference) were communists. The authorization was for 30 days and thus expired shortly before the assassination. However, it opened the floodgates for FBI surveillance of King that was to last until his death.

If anything was preoccupying Kennedy more on 22 November than the civil rights issue and its effect on his prospects for re-election, it was probably the worsening situation in Vietnam. During his presidency, the US military commitment to resisting communist insurgency in South Vietnam had risen from 875 'advisers' to 16,263. The American death toll was also rising, to a total of 77 in 1963. It was already becoming obvious that the only alternative to escalating US military involvement was to pull out, a step which Kennedy could not seriously contemplate.

The official justification for the presence of United States military forces in South Vietnam was that they had been invited there to help the government of Ngo Dinh

## Racial attitudes

At the time of Kennedy's death, the current issue of *Newsweek* carried a survey of racial attitudes in the United States. It made grim reading for proponents of racial equality.

A solid 20 to 25 percent of white Americans were in favour of effective apartheid — they objected to sitting next to a black person on a bus or at a lunch counter, or working with a black colleague, or having their child sit in the same classroom with a black child.

Beyond this substantial core of implacable racism — strongest, of course, in the South — there was deep and widespread prejudice on many issues throughout white America. For example, more than half of whites said they would object to a black family moving in next door — as one woman commented, 'We don't hate niggers. We just don't want them near us.' Almost half of whites were upset at the notion of their child bringing a black schoolfriend round for supper, and a massive 90 per cent said they would be opposed to their teenage son or daughter dating a black teenager.

More than one in three white Americans stated they believed blacks to be innately inferior; half believed blacks had less native intelligence than whites; and around two-thirds thought blacks lacked ambition, had loose morals, and smelt bad. Martin Luther King Jr had a lot of work to do.

**Influential members of the black civil rights movement met at the Hotel Roosevelt in early 1963. Under the umbrella of the National Association for the Advancement of Colored People, the campaign sought to increase the level of voter registration amongst the blacks of the southern states and remove segregation from the nation's schools. Amongst those present was, third from right, Martin Luther King. *The Hulton-Deutsch Collection Ltd***

***Above:*** **South Vietnamese troops patrol the rice paddies in 1963, accompanied by a US adviser, right. Although American losses in Vietnam were still low at this time — only one or two Americans were dying in combat each week — the situation was deteriorating rapidly.** ***The Hulton-Deutsch Collection Ltd***

***Above right:*** **Three weeks before Kennedy's death, the President was caught up in a new crisis when the leader of South Vietnam, Ngo Dinh Diem, was assassinated after a military coup on 2 November 1963. It was widely believed that Kennedy had backed the overthrow of Diem.** ***The Hulton-Deutsch Collection Ltd***

***Right:*** **The leader of North Vietnam was Ho Chi Minh. An inspirational leader, he would not live to see the North achieve ultimate victory.**

Diem. By September 1963, however, Diem had become an unpopular liability. A catholic dictator, he was waging open war on his country's Buddhist population. The Buddhist response included monks burning themselves to death in the street, in front of the world's TV cameras. These images shocked America. On 2 September, Kennedy told Walter Cronkite on CBS: 'I don't think the war can be won unless the people support the effort, and in my opinion, in the last two months the government has gotten out of touch with the people.' For Diem, the writing was on the wall.

A group of Saigon generals were made aware that if they carried out a coup against Diem, they could count on American support.

After much procrastination, they launched their coup on 1 November, and the following day Diem and his brother Nhu were captured and killed. Kennedy's special advisor, Arthur Schlesinger Jr., stated that 'it was no part of our plan, or expectations, that Diem and his brother would be murdered.' Yet Kennedy was at least implicated by tacit collusion in the slaying of an allied head of state less than three weeks before his own assassination.

By backing the generals' coup, the Americans effectively took control of South Vietnam. The future escalation of US involvement would be based on 'invitations' from governments that were no more than puppets of American military and economic power.

One school of thought about the Kennedy

assassination holds that the President was killed because the military-industrial complex wanted to stop him pulling out of Vietnam. But there has never been any evidence that Kennedy had such an intention.

Ironically, Kennedy intended to talk about Vietnam in his lunchtime speech at the Dallas Trade Mart, at the end of the motorcade through the city on 22 November. His speech was to refer to the military intervention in Southeast Asia as a 'painful, risky and costly effort', but a task 'we dare not weary of', since Americans were 'the watchmen on the walls of world freedom.' It was a speech he would never deliver.

# Four minute warning

Despite the signature of a treaty banning nuclear tests in the atmosphere (5 August 1963), the United States and the Soviet Union remained locked in a potentially disastrous nuclear confrontation. The nuclear balance in November 1963, according to the Institute for Stategic Studies, was definitely in the Americans' favour. They had 475 intercontinental ballistic missiles (ICBMs) as against 100 for the Soviets, 1,300 strategic bombers compared with 200 Soviet aircraft capable of attacking the United States, and 10 Polaris submarines with 16 missiles apiece, whereas the Soviet Union had as yet no submarines with nuclear missiles on board.

The United States' key nuclear delivery system at this time was still the B-52 bomber (as represented in Stanley Kubrick's *Dr Strangelove*), but Minuteman and Polaris missiles were rapidly taking over. A ring of early-warning radar stations had recently been constructed in Britain and Canada to give the United States time for a retaliatory strike in case of a surprise Soviet attack; everyone in Britain believed they knew how long they would have to live if there was a warning of a nuclear attack: precisely four minutes.

***Above:*** **The early 1960s was marked in Britain by the rise of the anti-nuclear movement. On 15 April 1963 protesters from the Campaign for Nuclear Disarmament marched along Kensington High Street *en route* to Trafalgar Square from Aldermaston. It is interesting to see how empty the streets were at the time; in the 1990s such a view would be dominated by huge numbers of private cars. On show at the Odeon across the road is Alexander Mackendrick's *Sammy Going South*, which featured Edward G. Robinson as a diamond mining outlaw. Mackendrick was also the director of the classic Ealing comedy *Whisky Galore!. The Hulton-Deutsch Collection Ltd***

***Left:*** **Also on the route from Aldermaston, where the Atomic Weapons Research body was based, to London was Reading. Here leading members of CND, including Jacquetta Hawkes (in the raincoat and scarf) and Canon Collins, parade through the town. Other influential figures in the anti-bomb movement included the philosopher Bertrand Russell and the politician Michael Foot. *The Hulton-Deutsch Collection Ltd***

## 'ICH BIN EIN BERLINER'

One of President Kennedy's most celebrated speeches was delivered from the balcony of the Schoneberg Rathaus, the seat of the West Berlin city government, during his last tour of Europe on 26 June 1963. It concluded:

'There are some who say that communism is the wave of the future. Let them come to Berlin. And there are some who say in Europe and elsewhere we can work with the communists. Let them come to Berlin. And there are even a few who say it is true that communism is an evil system, but it permits us to make economic progress. Lasst sie nach Berlin kommen. Let them

come to Berlin... All free men, wherever they may live, are citizens of Berlin, and, therefore, as a free man, I take pride in the words "Ich bin ein Berliner".'

It is unfortunate that Kennedy's final rhetorical flourish, 'I am a Berliner', had an ambiguity to it — since 'Berliner' is also the German name for a jam-filled doughnut

***Left:*** **One of Kennedy's most famous overseas tours during his short presidency was that to Berlin in June 1963. The East German authorities hung large red drapes on the Brandenburg Gate so that Kennedy could not see into East Berlin, nor be seen from the Communist part of the divided city.**
***The Hulton-Deutsch Collection Ltd***

***Below:*** **President Kennedy is seen in the company of Berlin's Mayor Willy Brandt and German Chancellor Konrad Adenauer on 26 June 1963. It was during this trip to Berlin that the US president uttered his immortal line: 'Ich bin ein Berliner!'.**
***The Hulton-Deutsch Collection Ltd***

## THE SPY PLANE

On the day of Kennedy's assassination, the newspapers were still covering the disappearance two days earlier of a U2 spyplane off the coast of Florida. Official sources described the aircraft as a W-U2, the extra initial standing for weather, claiming that the plane's mission was only meteorological. This was not widely believed, a likelier explanation being that the U2 had been on a reconnaissance mission over Cuba.

The U2, which could fly at a height of 85,000 feet, had been introduced in 1956 for espionage on the Soviet Union. In four years the aircraft successfully conducted 13 flights over Soviet territory, photographing military installations, until one piloted by Gary Powers was shot down by a Soviet missile on 1 May 1960. The U2 also played a key role in the 1962 Cuban Missile Crisis. Aerial reconnaissance photographs taken by U2 pilot Major Rudolf Anderson triggered the crisis by confirming the construction of nuclear missile installations on the island, and the shooting down of Anderson's plane on another mission over Cuba at the height of the confrontation almost precipitated open war.

After these excitements, the U2 gradually faded from military importance as satellite surveillance took over its role. The aircraft was withdrawn from service in 1976.

# 3

# ASSASSINATION

When the first rifle shot sounded across Dealey Plaza, it was 12.30 p.m. central standard time (cst) in Dallas, Texas. In California, it was 10.30 a.m. pacific standard time (pst). In Washington, D.C., and in New York it was 1.30 p.m. eastern standard time (est) on a day of cool wind and bright, warm sunlight. In London it was 6.30 p.m. and already dark, a mild but blustery evening. As author William Manchester has pointed out, when Abraham Lincoln was assassinated almost a century earlier, consideration of time zones had been irrelevant. But the world had arrived in the era of instantaneous communications, and the events of 22 November were experienced as they happened by people across the globe. So Americans followed the

**It is 12.30pm on Elm Street, Dallas, and President Kennedy has been shot.** ***The Hulton-Deutsch Collection Ltd***

The moment after Kennedy's assassination: Mrs Jacqueline Kennedy leans over her stricken husband whilst a secret serviceman leaps on to the rear bumper. From the centre of Dallas the president's car rushed to the Parkland Hospital where he was pronounced dead in an operating theatre at about 1pm. *The Hulton-Deutsch Collection Ltd*

death of the President and its aftermath through the afternoon, the British through the evening, the Russians through the night.

What exactly happened in Dallas during the five seconds it took to murder the president has remained unclear ever since. We know what the event looked like in awful detail from the 152 frames of Abe Zapruder's 8mm amateur movie (although the public did not see this at the time, since all the television networks considered the pictures too violent and tasteless to broadcast; stills from the film were printed in *Life* magazine, but the moving film was not shown on television until 1975). We know that Kennedy was hit by two shots, one that wounded him in the neck and back, and a second that blew away the side of his head. We know that Governor Connally was also wounded in the back and wrist. We know that Jacqueline Kennedy attempted to scramble out of the back of the car, screaming: 'My God, what are they doing? They've killed Jack, they've killed my husband ... Jack, Jack!' And that Governor Connally collapsed into his wife's lap, crying out: 'My God, they're trying to kill us all.' Beyond this, little about the assassination is certain.

In the confusion of the moment, few of those present had a clear idea of what had happened. Railmen standing on the bridge in front of the limousine thought that shots had been fired from behind a wooden fence on a grassy knoll overlooking Dealey Plaza. Other witnesses believed they had seen a rifleman in the Book Depository building, though some placed the man in a different location to the sixth floor window from which Oswald is supposed to have fired the fatal shots.

To anyone more than a hundred yards or so from the incident, it was unclear that anything dramatic had happened at all. Tom Wicker of the *New York Times*, who was travelling in a press bus in the motorcade about ten cars behind the president, has narrated how a journalist at the front of the bus reported that the president's car had sped off — but 'that could have happened if someone had thrown a tomato at the president'. The reporters drove on to the Trade Mart where

Johnson Takes Nation's Helm, Pages 4 and 5

The Dallas Morning News

John F. Kennedy Life History, Pages 16 and 17

VOL. 115—NO. 54 TELEPHONE: Riverside 7-4611 DALLAS, TEXAS, SATURDAY, NOVEMBER 23, 1963—50 PAGES IN 4 SECTIONS ★★★★ PRICE 5 CENTS

# KENNEDY SLAIN ON DALLAS STREET

★ ★ ★ ★ ★ ★ ★ ★ ★ ★ ★ ★ ★ ★ ★ ★

# JOHNSON BECOMES PRESIDENT

## Receives Oath on Aircraft

By ROBERT E. BASKIN
Washington Bureau of The News

In a solemn and sorrowful hour, with a nation mourning its dead President, Lyndon B. Johnson Friday took the oath of office as the 36th chief executive of the United States.

Following custom, the oath-taking took place quickly—only an hour and a half after the assassination of President Kennedy.

Federal Judge Sarah T. Hughes of Dallas administered the oath in a hurriedly arranged ceremony at 2:39 p.m. aboard Air Force 1, the presidential plane that brought Kennedy on his ill-fated Texas trip and on which his body was taken back to Washington.

Mrs. Johnson and Mrs. Kennedy, her stocking still flecked with blood from the assassination, flanked the vice-president as he raised his right hand in the forward compartment of the presidential jetliner at Love Field. About 25 White House staff members and friends were present as Johnson intoned the familiar oath:

"I do solemnly swear that I will perform the duties of President of the United States to the best of my ability, and defend, protect and preserve the Constitution of the United States."

The 55-year-old Johnson, the first Texan ever to become President, turned and kissed his wife on the cheek, giving her shoulders a squeeze. Then he put his arm around Mrs. Kennedy, kissing her gently on her right cheek.

Mrs. Kennedy, in tears, was wearing the same bright pink suit she wore on the fatal ride, a ride in which she had been widly acclaimed by friendly, cheering crowds in Dallas before rifle shots rang out and the President collapsed in the seat of the car beside her.

Johnson had deliberately delayed the ceremony to give Kennedy's widow time to compose herself for one of the gruelling aspects of her husband's assassination.

CONTINUED ON PAGE 15

*Lyndon B. Johnson*

## *Gov. Connally Resting Well*

By MIKE QUINN

Gov. John Connally — felled Friday by a sniper's bullet in the back—rested in "quite satisfactory" condition late Friday night at Parkland Hospital following nearly four hours of surgery in the afternoon.

An aide for the governor reported at 10:30 p.m. that the governor was asleep and resting comfortably following the incident which claimed President Kennedy's life.

Meanwhile, Dr. Tom Shires, chief of surgeons at University of Texas Southwestern Medical School, said Connally barely missed a fatal wound:

"After consulting with Mrs. Connally and others on the scene, the consensus is that the governor was quite fortunate that he turned to see what happened to the President. If he had not turned to his right, there is a good chance he probably would have been shot through the heart—as it was, the bullet caused a tangential wound."

Dr. Shires rushed to Dallas by Air Force jet after word of the shooting was flashed.

Connally was operated on by Dr. Robert R. Shaw, thoracic

CONTINUED ON PAGE 2.

## Impact Shattering To World Capitals

By the Associated Press

Word of President Kennedy's assassination struck the world's capitals with shattering impact, leaving heads of state and the man in the street stunned and grief-stricken.

While messages of condolence poured into the White House from presidents, premiers and crowned heads, the little people of many lands reacted with numbed disbelief.

Pubs in London and cafes in Paris fell silent, as the news came over radio and television.

**IN MOSCOW,** a Russian girl walked weeping along the street.

At U.N. headquarters in New York, delegates of 11 nations bowed their heads in a moment of silence.

In Buenos Aires, newspapers sounded sirens reserved for news of the utmost gravity.

Britain's Prime Minister Douglas-Home sent condolences, and Sir Winston Churchill branded the slaying a monstrous act.

"The loss to the United States and to the world is incalculable," Sir Winston declared. "Those who come after Mr. Kennedy must strive the more to achieve the ideals of world peace and human happiness and dignity to which his presidency was dedicated."

Douglas-Home issued this terse statement:

"The Prime Minister has learned with the most profound shock and horror of the death

CONTINUED ON PAGE 2.

## Pro-Communist Charged With Act

A sniper shot and killed President John F. Kennedy on the streets of Dallas Friday. A 24-year-old pro-Communist who once tried to defect to Russia was charged with the murder shortly before midnight.

Kennedy was shot about 12:20 p.m. Friday at the foot of Elm Street as the Presidential car entered the approach to the Triple Underpass. The President died in a sixth-floor surgery room at Parkland Hospital about 1 p.m., though doctors said there was no chance for him to live when he reached the hospital.

Within two hours, Vice-President Lyndon Johnson was sworn in as the nation's 36th President inside the presidential plane before departing for Washington.

The gunman also seriously wounded Texas Gov. John Connally, who was riding with the President.

### *Four Hours in Surgery*

Connally spent four hours on an operating table, but his condition was reported as "quite satisfactory" at midnight.

The assassin, firing from the sixth floor of the Texas School Book Depository Building near the Triple Underpass sent a Mauser 6.5 rifle bullet smashing into the President's head.

An hour after the President died, police hauled the 24-year-old suspect, Lee Harvey Oswald, out of an Oak Cliff movie house.

He had worked for a short time at the depository, and police had encountered him while searching the building shortly after the assassination. They turned him loose when he was identified as an employe but put out a pickup order on him when he failed to report for a work roll call.

He also was accused of killing a Dallas policeman, J. D. Tippit, whose body was found during the vast manhunt for the President's assassin.

Oswald, who has an extensive pro-Communist background, four years ago renounced his American citizenship in Russia and tried to become a Russian citizen. Later, he returned to this country.

### *Friendly Crowd Cheered Kennedy*

Shockingly, the President was shot after driving the length of Main Street through a crowd termed the largest and friendliest of his 2-day Texas visit. It was a good-natured crowd that surged out from the curbs almost against the swiftly moving presidential car. The protective bubble had been removed from the official convertible.

Mrs. Connally, who occupied one of the two jump seats in the car, turned to the President a few moments before and remarked, "You can't say Dallas wasn't friendly to you."

At Fort Worth, Kennedy had just delivered one of the most well-received speeches of his ca-

CONTINUED ON PAGE 2.

## *FUNERAL FOR PRESIDENT WILL BE HELD ON MONDAY*

WASHINGTON (AP)—President Kennedy's funeral will be held Monday at St. Matthews Roman Catholic Cathedral, the White House announced Friday night.

The body of the slain President will lie in repose at the White House Saturday and will lie in state in the rotunda of the Capitol on Sunday and Monday.

The President's body will be taken a couple of miles to the cathedral at 11 a.m. (EST) Monday. There, Richard Cardinal Cushing, Archbishop of Boston and close friend of the Kennedy family, will celebrate a pontifical requiem Mass at noon.

Acting White House Press Secretary Andrew T. Hatcher said he did not know where Kennedy will be buried. There has been one report, still unconfirmed, that burial would be in the family plot in Brookline, Mass.

The President's body will be moved from the White House in an official cortege to the Capitol rotunda at 1 p.m. Sunday. This ceremony will be attended by members of the

CONTINUED ON PAGE 12.

*John F. Kennedy*

*GRAY CLOUDS WENT AWAY*

## Day Began as Auspiciously As Any in Kennedy's Career

*(Robert E. Baskin, chief of the Washington Bureau of The News, was one of four persons representing the world press in the motorcade which resulted in the President's assassination. This is his account of what happened.)*

By ROBERT E. BASKIN
Washington Bureau of The News

It was a day that started as auspiciously as any in the career of John F. Kennedy.

When we boarded the Presidential jetliner, Air Force One, at Fort Worth at midmorning, the White House party was in high spirits. The Fort Worth welcome had been a tremendous one. Shortly before the 15-minute flight to Love Field, ugly gray clouds were swept away by a brisk breeze. The sun was out, and the Texas sky was a vivid blue.

President and Mrs. Kennedy, she strikingly attired in a pink suit with a pert matching hat, made an instant hit at Love Field as they shook hands with hundreds of persons along the fence line.

Then the last journey began.

The big open Lincoln car moved out smoothly, carrying Mr. and Mrs. Kennedy and Gov. John Connally and his wife, Nellie.

Three cars back was the press pool car, in which three other newspapermen and I rode. Just ahead of us were Dallas Mayor and Mrs. Earle Cabell and Rep. Ray Roberts of McKinney.

Malcolm Kilduff, assistant presidential press secretary, was with us, and as we moved into the heart of the city Kilduff expressed elation over the friendly nature of the welcome and the great outpouring of people.

Everyone in the press car agreed it was one of the most cordial receptions the President had received in quite a while.

Buoyed by the cheers of the multitudes on Main Street, our motorcade moved on past the courthouse. Then came the approach to the Triple Underpass, with the leading cars picking up speed as the crowd thinned out somewhat. Over to our right loomed the gaunt structure labeled the Texas State School Book Depositary.

It was 12:30 p.m.

The sharp crack of a rifle rang out. But at that moment we couldn't believe it was just that. "What the hell was that?" someone in our car asked.

Then there were two more shots—measured carefully.

We saw people along the street diving for the ground.

CONTINUED ON PAGE 2.

they were to cover the president's lunchtime speech, and it was there that they learned through a phone call that the President had been shot and was at Parkland Hospital.

Less out of touch were the journalists in the press 'pool' car. They were only about five vehicles behind the president in the motorcade and heard the shots. While journalists in the press buses drove on to the Trade Mart, the pool car sped after the presidential limousine to the hospital.

One of those in the pool car was Merriman Smith of United Press International (UPI). Thus the first news of the assassination arrived in newspaper offices and radio and television newsrooms across the world through the UPI network. Merriman Smith was equipped with a radiotelephone. Aware that shots had been fired, but having no idea whether the president had been hit, he contacted the Dallas UPI office from the car as it raced toward the hospital. At 12.34 Dallas interrupted transmission of news from a Minneapolis murder trial with this message: DALLAS, NOV. 22 (UPI) — THREE SHOTS WERE FIRED AT PRESIDENT KENNEDY'S MOTORCADE TODAY IN DOWNTOWN DALLAS.

After a brief interruption, the message continued to clatter out of the teletype machines: NO CASUALTIES WERE REPORTED. THE INCIDENT OCCURRED NEAR THE COUNTY SHERIFF'S OFFICE ON MAIN STREET, JUST EAST OF AN UNDERPASS LEADING TOWARD THE TRADE MART WHERE THE PRESIDENT WAS TO MA

At this point the message broke off in mid word, because Smith had arrived at the hospital, found out what had happened, and phoned the tragic news through to the Dallas office. The operator immediately transmitted: FLASH KENNEDY SERIOUSLY WOUNDED PERHAPS SERIOUSLY PERHAPS FATALLY BY ASSASSINS BULLET.

It was nine minutes after the assassination and Dallas had become the focal point of the world. At 12.36 cst the ABC network broke into local radio broadcasts to relay the first UPI message. Four minutes later, CBS interrupted its lunchtime soap opera *As the World Turns* for Walter Cronkite to announce: 'In Dallas, Texas, three shots were fired at President Kennedy's motorcade. The first reports say that the President was "seriously wounded".' Cronkite, who had only become the front man for CBS news the previous year, had fortuitously decided not to go out for lunch; his appearances this day were to help make him a legend in US broadcasting.

The front runners in the highly competitive field of US television news were NBC with their two-man presentation team, David Brinkley in Washington and Chet Huntley in New York. They were tied into AP instead of UPI, however, and were last to respond to the news. Huntley interrupted *Bachelor Father* to make the announcement in New York, but NBC in Washington was still broadcasting a fashion show when most of America already knew a tragedy was under way. According to subsequent surveys, 68 per cent of Americans — about 75 million people — had heard the news by 1.00 cst, 30 minutes after the shooting. Roughly half of them got their information from radio and television, the other half by word of mouth. Indeed, almost everyone who got the message from the media went straight away to tell someone else, by phone or face to face. Phone lines were jammed and operators had to refuse calls. If there was no friend or acquaintance contactable, people told the first person they could find — one in ten Americans heard the news from a total stranger.

When the first news broke, the majority of US television viewers (in the sexually segregated world of 1963) were housewives, watching the downmarket afternoon soap operas. Other people were more likely to hear it on the radio, especially their car radios as they drove to or from home at the beginning or end of their lunch break. Nancy Reagan, for example, was driving down San Vicente Boulevard in Los Angeles when the barely credible news flash broke into the programme she was listening to (it was a moment she would remember vividly when she heard that her own husband had been shot 18 years later). Many drivers pulled into the side of the road to listen. Senator Hubert Humphrey sat in his car in Massachusetts Avenue, Washington, cursing the right-wing extremists he was sure had done the deed. Other people got out to talk to passers-by or other motorists. Those at lunch rushed to any available set as the news spread. Soon about two-thirds of the nation were huddled around radios and televisions.

***The Dallas Morning News* treated the assassination in dignified fashion on 23 November.**

Around the world there was much mourning for the demise of a youthful and popular politician. In Britain, Sir Winston Churchill, then in his late 80s, commented 'The loss to the United States and the world is incalculable. Those who come after Mr Kennedy must strive the more to achieve the ideals of world peace and human happiness and dignity to which his presidency was dedicated.' Flags on official buildings were flown at half mast — as at the US embassy in London — where people queued to sign a book of condolences. *The Hulton-Deutsch Collection Ltd*

In Dallas all was confusion. At the hospital rumours were rife as journalists battled for phone lines. AP news agency announced that Vice-President Johnson had also been wounded — because he had been seen to rub his arm on arriving at the hospital. Television viewers learned that a priest had arrived at the hospital; they did not learn immediately that the last rites had been administered. At 1.00 CST Kennedy was pronounced dead, but it was another half an hour before White House press secretary Mac Kilduff confirmed to reporters what they had already guessed. At 1.35 CST, Walter Cronkite, visibly moved, announced the death of the President to the American people.

*The New York Times* described the immediate reaction: 'The cry rang across the city, echoing again and again: "Is it true?"... Women wept and men wept. A refusal to believe the report of the assassination was the immediate reaction, but swiftly came horror, then anguish, and then among many... deep anger.' Disc jockey Paul Gambaccini, then at high school in Westport, Connecticut, remembers the news coming through on the school intercom: 'After the announcement, the girl sitting behind me, Mary Ann Golden, burst into tears. "Why do they always kill the great people?" she sobbed.' British diplomat Sir Brian Urquhart did not hear the news when it was first broadcast because he was in a taxi traveling from Idlewild Airport (soon to be Kennedy Airport) to his apartment in Manhattan. When he arrived at the apartment building, to his astonishment he found all the doormen were in tears.

Journalist George Barrett tells how one driver stopped his car right in the middle of dense city traffic and walked over to a sidewalk luncheonette to ask whether the news was true. 'The motorist returned to his car, slipped under the wheel and sat, motionless and staring. Horns blared, then went soundless, as word of the President's death filtered from driver to driver.'

In the highest echelons of government, there were fears of a coup or a nuclear attack. US armed forces were put on the alert and security in Washington was tightened. The capital was strangely empty of top level politicians — Secretary of State Dean Rusk was on an aircraft over the Pacific with five other members of Kennedy's Cabinet, on their way to visit Japan. Secretary of Defense Robert S. McNamara took control at the Pentagon and kept nerves calm. In Dallas, Vice-President Johnson had been whisked away from the hospital to the Presidental aircraft at Love Field, where he could be sworn in as Kennedy's successor (once they managed to locate the text of the oath) and flown back to take over in Washington.

Panicky rumours continued to circulate: AP reported that a secret service agent and a policeman had been shot and killed near the scene of the assassination. But real

SEE THE TALBOT FORD & LEEBRET XMAS BARGAINS ON PAGE 15.

DAILY SKETCH

Saturday, November 23, 1963 Price Threepence *** WEATHER: Sunny spells

NEVER DRAIN FORLIFE

WAITING GUNMAN HID ON 5th FLOOR, ATE FRIED CHICKEN

KENNEDY ASSASSIN: RED SUSPECT HELD

Lee Oswald

'Married to a Russian'

By HENRY THODY
NEW YORK, Midnight

AN American Communist who once defected to Russia and who married a Russian girl was seized by G-men tonight after the assassination of President Kennedy.

He is the No. 1 suspect in the massive dragnet which went out after a killer, hiding in a fifth-floor room shot down the President as he was riding in a motor-cade procession.

CORNERED IN A CINEMA

The man is 24-year-old ex-Marine Lee Harvey Oswald, who last year was granted permission to return to the United States from Moscow after he was refused permission to take Russian citizenship.

He is also reported to be chairman of an organisation which calls itself "Fair Play For Cuba."

Oswald, father of a year-old baby girl, was arrested in Dallas, Texas, after a chase in which a policeman was shot dead. He was cornered in a cinema and hauled screaming into a squad car.

He was said to have been an employee in the building where police found the rifle which killed President Kennedy and seriously wounded the Governor.

➡ Back Page

DRAMA IN PICTURES —Centre Pages

'No! No!' cries Jackie as bullets rip into the car

Moment of horror . . . Bullets crash. A guard leaps on to the President's car and Mrs. Kennedy bends over her husband. She cradled his head in her arms crying "No! No!" Twenty five minutes later he was dead.

**The front page of the tabloid *Daily Sketch* for 23 November reported both the assassination of Kennedy and the arrest of the suspected assassin Lee Harvey Oswald. Much was made of Oswald's connection with the Soviet Union.**

CLASSIFIED
GREEN GODDESS
HER FAVOURITE DRINK
POOLS CHECK
600 GEORGE COHEN'S for PLANT and MACHINERY
Evening Standard
The assassination of the President —Special memorial edition
LAST GOOD-BYE
POOLS CHECK
RESULTS
COUPON CHECK
WINNING LINES
FIXED ODDS
SCOTTISH LEAGUE DIV. I
SCOTTISH LEAGUE DIV. II
AMATEUR INTERNATIONAL
'A Communist'
Prince Philip and Premier to fly to U.S.
Late scorers
Gregg breaks bone
The man a bullet puts in the White House
PAGE SEVEN
Ladybird—a good head for business
Broken bottles in Washington
By Jean Campbell
PAGE THREE
Randolph Churchill

events unfolded in an unsurpassably dramatic manner, some of them known to the public, others not. There was a bitter and unseemly dispute over possession of the President's corpse, won by the Secret Service over protests from local officials; the body was taken to Air Force 1, along with Jacqueline Kennedy. Still in her cheerful pink dress, her stockings spattered with her husband's blood, she stood alongside Johnson as he was sworn in as President at 2.38 cst Elsewhere in Dallas, a policeman, J. D. Tippit, had been shot and a man arrested for his murder in the Texas Theatre movie house. At 3.15 cst the name Lee Harvey Oswald was first broadcast to America. Within minutes the connection between the death of officer Tippit and the Kennedy assassination had been made and journalists began to uncover Oswald's bizarre and incriminating background.

As events unfolded, normal life across the United States came to a halt. Schools were closed and their pupils sent home. Many offices and shops closed also, or were half deserted. All flags were lowered. Authorities began to announce from all sides the cancellation of entertainments, from symphony concerts to the next day's Harvard-Yale football game. There was an unnatural hush on city streets and church bells tolled.

Not everyone, of course, was grief-stricken. Kennedy's enemies on the right were indifferent or triumphant. In one famous incident, children at a Dallas school applauded when their teacher told them of the President's death. The city's high schools pointedly did not cancel floodlit

***Above:*** **The *Evening Standard* reported Jacqueline Kennedy's final goodbye to her dead husband: 'She clutches the hand of her brother-in-law, Attorney General Robert Kennedy, as she watches her husband's coffin being placed in a Navy ambulance. Mrs Kennedy said her last good-bye with a kiss. She slipped her wedding ring on her husband's hand.'**

***Far right:*** **All over the world there was shock over the assassination. In Moscow, for example, Khrushchev visited the US embassy to pay his condolences. 'Kennedy ermordet' (Kennedy murdered) was the stark headline of the *Hamburger Abendblatt* on 23 November.**

## Hoover goes to the races

At 1.45 est in Washington, Attorney General Robert Kennedy was at home finishing a poolside lunch with New York federal attorney Robert Morgenthau when he was told there was an urgent call for him from FBI chief J. Edgar Hoover. This was most unusual; the two men were on such bad terms that they never spoke unless it was absolutely necessary. When Bobby picked up the phone, Hoover said drily: 'I have news for you. The president's been shot.' Morgenthau saw Bobby Kennedy put his hand to his mouth as if to smother an exclamation of horror. Then Bobby said: 'Jack's been shot. It may be fatal.'

Hoover rang again 30 minutes later to say that the president was dead, but Bobby had already heard the tragic news from the White House staff. During the two calls he made, Hoover attempted no expression of sympathy, not even the most formal condolences. Robert Kennedy later remarked acidly that the FBI chief's tone was 'not quite as excited as if he were reporting the fact that he had found a Communist on the faculty of Howard University'.

The following day, when all America was prostrate with grief and shock, and the whole nation was obsessed with the question who had killed the president and why, Hoover went to the races with his friend Clyde Tolson. For the head of the FBI, it was a Saturday like any other.

34 91 91 und für Anzeigen 34 10 15

# Hamburger  Abendblatt

Das Wetter am Wochenende
Wechselnd bewölkt, einzelne Schauer, bis 8 Grad

Nr. 273 / Jahrgang 16 / Einzelpreis 50 Pf / C 3590 A · UNABHÄNGIG · Hamburger Fremdenblatt · ÜBERPARTEILICH · Hamburg, Sbd./Stg., den 23./24. November 1963

## Freitag, 19.30 MEZ — Tatort Dallas in Texas

# Kennedy ermordet

## Kopfschuß aus dem Hinterhalt

## Frau Kennedy blieb unverletzt

## Johnson neuer US-Präsident

**19.28 Uhr:** John F. Kennedy und der Gouverneur von Texas, John Connally, fahren durch Dallas. Die Bevölkerung winkt dem Präsidenten zu.

Eigener Dienst-ap-dpa-upi

**New York, 23. November**

**John F. Kennedy ist tot. Amerikas 46jähriger Präsident ist durch gezielten Kopfschuß eines Fanatikers ermordet worden.**

**Mit Erschütterung stehen Amerika und die ganze Weltöffentlichkeit vor dieser Nachricht, die am Freitagabend über den Erdball ging, die aber den Menschen noch immer unfaßbar ist.**

Nachdem sich die erste Verwirrung gelegt und die sich zunächst widersprechenden Nachrichten geklärt haben, ergibt sich folgender Tatbestand:

**Präsident Kennedy befand sich in Dallas in Texas mit einer Wagenkolonne auf der Fahrt zu einer Kundgebung, als um 19.25 Uhr MEZ aus dem oberen Stockwerk eines Warenhauses drei Schüsse auf ihn abgegeben wurden.**

Die Mordwaffe war ein Jagdgewehr mit Zielfernrohr.

**Der Präsident wurde durch einen Kopfschuß getroffen und brach sofort zusammen.**

Mrs. Jacqueline Kennedy, die im Auto ihres Mannes saß, schrie auf: „Nein, nein, nein!" Sie warf sich über den Körper ihres Mannes, als ob sie ihn schützen wolle. In wenigen Sekunden waren ihre Kleider vom Blut durchtränkt.

**Zwei Schüsse trafen den Gouverneur von Texas, Connally.**

Die Autokolonne war gerade im Begriff, in eine dreifache Straßenunterführung einzufahren, als die Schüsse abgegeben wurden.

Der Täter hat sich nach den Ermittlungen des FBI wahrscheinlich schon einen ganzen Tag vor der

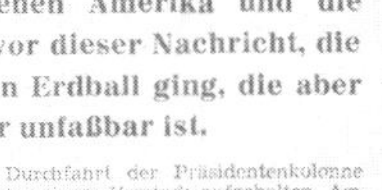

Durchfahrt der Präsidentenkolonne in seinem Versteck aufgehalten. Am Tatort wurden außer der Mordwaffe auch noch die Reste einer Mahlzeit sichergestellt. Außerdem fand die Polizei drei leere Patronenhülsen sowie ein Papierknäuel, das wahrscheinlich als Unterlage für das Gewehr benutzt wurde.

**Nach den Schrecksekunden dirigierte die Leibwache des Präsidenten den Wagen verzweifelt in das Parkland-Krankenhaus in Dallas. Schon kurz nach 19.30 Uhr MEZ erhielt Kennedy, der noch bei Bewußtsein war, eine Bluttransfusion.**

Der Arzt Dr. Malcolm Perrey, der sofort die Behandlung übernahm, alarmierte alle Ärzte, die erreichbar waren. Die Ärzte versuchten eine Atemmassage. Ein Lachgasäthergerät wurde zu Hilfe genommen. Als äußerstes Mittel versuchten die Ärzte einen Luftröhrenschnitt.

**Es war zu spät. Fast genau um 20 Uhr MEZ schloß Kennedy die Augen. Um 20.35 MEZ gab das Weiße Haus in Washington amtlich den Tod des Präsidenten bekannt.**

Bei der Verfolgung des Attentäters durch die Straßen von Dallas wurde vor einem Kino ein Kriminalbeamter

(Fortsetzung auf Seite 2)

### Die Kinder wissen noch nichts

Deutsche Presse-Agentur

**Washington, 23. November**

**Den beiden Kindern des Präsidentenpaares, der fünfjährigen Caroline und dem fast dreijährigen John, ist — wie ein Sprecher des Weißen Hauses mitteilte — bisher noch nichts von dem tragischen Tod ihres Vaters gesagt worden. Der Sprecher fügte hinzu, die Kinder würden im Weißen Haus von ihrer Nurse betreut.**

### Für drei Tage halbmast

Deutsche Presse-Agentur

**Bonn, 22. November**

**Unmittelbar nach Bekanntwerden der Todesnachricht hat Bundesinnenminister Höcherl am Freitagabend angeordnet, daß sämtliche Bundesbehörden von sofort an halbmast flaggen. Für Hamburg hat der Senat für drei Tage Halbmast-Beflaggung angeordnet.**

Auch die Gebäude der Bundeswehr werden die Flaggen am Sonnabend auf halbmast setzen. Diese Anordnung traf der Staatssekretär im Bundesverteidigungsministerium, Hopf, an Stelle von Verteidigungsminister von Hassel, der auf der Fahrt nach New York ist.

**19.31 Uhr:** Drei Schüsse haben den Präsidenten getroffen. Frau Jacqueline beugt sich über den Schwerverletzten. Ein unbekannter Mann ist auf die Stoßstange des Präsidentenwagens gesprungen. Die Wagenkolonne setzt die Fahrt fort.

**19.32 Uhr:** Entsetzte Menschen, die noch nicht begriffen haben, was geschehen ist, haben sich aus Furcht vor weiteren Schüssen auf die Erde geworfen. Nur ein paar Fotografen versuchen, die Szene festzuhalten.

football games to be held that Friday evening. Among radical blacks sceptical of Kennedy's commitment to civil rights and accustomed to being the victims of violence that went unpunished, there was also much cynicism about the general outpouring of grief.

But of the genuineness of the majority response there can be no question. Sociological surveys carried out after the event confirmed, as Wilbur Schramm writes, 'feelings rolled over the nation in an immense tide. The most common reactions were to be sorry for Mrs Kennedy and the children, sorry that a vital young man should be killed at the height of his powers, ashamed that such a thing could happen in our country,... and angry that someone could have done such a deed.' For many these feelings 'were followed by physical symptoms such as weeping, tenseness, sleeplessness, fatigue, or loss of appetite'.

Why was the reaction so much stronger than we suspect it would be if President Clinton were shot? The intensity of the response has often been attributed to the impact of television, but there is no evidence that people who followed what happened on the radio were any less emotionally involved. Obviously, the carefully projected image of Kennedy as a warm family man, with his pretty wife and two young children, helped engage people's

## 'THIS IS GOING TO HAPPEN TO ME'

Civil rights leader Martin Luther King Jr. was at his home in Atlanta, Georgia, when the news came through on television that Kennedy had been shot. He called his wife Coretta Scott King to join him, and they prayed for the President's survival.

According to Coretta, when it was announced that the President had died, Martin was silent for a while: ' Finally he said, "This is what is going to happen to me also. I keep telling you, this is a sick society." I was not able to say anything. I had no word to comfort my husband. I could not say, "It won't happen to you." I felt he was right. It was a painfully agonising silence. I moved closer to him and gripped his hand in mine.' Martin Luther King was assassinated on 4 April 1968.

**As a mark of respect footballers playing in league games on the Saturday wore black armbands and stood in silence at the start of the match. Arsenal, seen closest to the camera in their traditional red and white strip, were to defeat Blackpool 5-3 at Highbury. Thirty years on the players would be wearing 'designer' kits, with logos and sponsors names emblazoned all over. Note also the lack of covered accommodation for the supporters. *The Hulton-Deutsch Collection Ltd***

feelings when disaster struck. But the mainspring of grief probably lay in the political dramas of the time. It was only a year since the Cuban Missile Crisis had brought anxiety about nuclear war to its peak, and two months since Martin Luther King's March on Washington had stung America to shame at its inequality and injustice. Consciously or not, Americans felt Kennedy was the hero who would shield them from a dangerous world outside and slay the country's dragons within. But the dragon had slain the hero, and the nation experienced the grief of the vulnerable and the unprotected.

At 6.05 est the presidential aircraft landed at Andrews Air Base. Bobby Kennedy and a small group of Kennedy associates and politicians had assembled there to meet it. Author Theodore H. White had flown down from New York; he later recalled: 'I cried and cried as they gently lifted the coffin out.' The Kennedys drove off with the dead President to Bethesda Naval Hospital; Johnson made a brief speech for the cameras — 'This is a sad time for all people. We have suffered a loss that cannot be weighed...' The millions of television viewers, observing the weary, time-corrupted features of the wily political fixer uttering these dignified platitudes, started adjusting to the notion that this was now the face of the President of the United States.

The first news of the events in Dallas reached Britain at 6.42 p.m., twelve

**Officers of the Coldstream Guards also wore black armbands for the changing of the guards ceremony at Buckingham Palace on 23 November. The Queen sent a message to Mrs Kennedy: 'I am so deeply distressed to learn of the tragic death of President Kennedy. My husband joins me in sending our heartfelt and sincere sympathy to you and your family. Elizabeth R'. *The Hulton-Deutsch Collection Ltd***

minutes after the fatal shots were fired. Patrick Morley, then the chief sub-editor in the BBC's radio newsroom at Broadcasting House, was struggling with 'one of those days when it's difficult to fill the bulletins'. Twenty years later Morley recalled his experience for the Observer: 'I asked the duty sub-editor if he had anything new for the 7 o'clock headlines; he hadn't. For the fifth time that day I said: "What we want is a really good story." A couple of minutes later the first Reuter flash arrived: 'President Kennedy shot at while riding in a motor convoy.' Almost immediately it was confirmed that Kennedy had been hit — the agency reported that a press photographer had seen blood on the President's head.

As in the United States, newsrooms burst into chaotic activity. Editors and journalists raced back to their desks from their early evening drinking haunts to follow the evolving tragedy on the agency tapes. News flash followed news flash until 7.22, when the BBC Monitoring Service picked up an announcement on Voice of America radio that Kennedy was dead. Since Voice of America was considered a semi-official mouthpiece for the United States government, no one had any doubt the news must be true.

The Granada pop show *Scene* — that evening starring, among others, the Rolling Stones — is usually credited with making the first announcement of the shooting on British television at around 6.50. The BBC delayed until 7.05, when about 1.9 million people were settling down for the *Tonight* programme, before announcer John Roberts broadcast the news that the President had been shot. Most of the 8 million ITV viewers had to wait until 7.17 — the commercial break in the popular game show *Take Your Pick* fronted by Michael Miles — before they received their first intimation of what was happening in Dallas.

At about 7.25, Roberts interrupted the *Tonight* programme again to tell viewers that the President was undergoing a blood transfusion. While Roberts was on the air, the Voice of America message came through and was passed to him. It was thus he who made the solemn statement: 'We regret to announce that President Kennedy is dead.' Five minutes later, the news was broadcast on the ITV network.

Many people, of course, in Britain as in the United States, heard the news on radio or by word of mouth. Labour politician Jim Callaghan, who had been re-elected to the Shadow Cabinet the previous day, was taking a holiday in Devon with his wife. Driving down a narrow country lane, he switched on the car radio and picked up the announcement of the assassination. 'I pulled into the side of the road and stopped,' he remembered, 'because the news was so overwhelming and the impact so stunning'. Jazz singer George Melly walked into a Hammersmith pub — 'not a posh public house' — and noticed everyone was looking depressed. Jokingly, he asked 'Who's dead?', and got an answer he was not expecting. Future politician and novelist Jeffrey Archer was attending a debate at the Oxford Student Union when he heard a rumour that Kennedy had been shot; initially at least he simply refused to believe it. Neil Kinnock, then a young Labour activist, was in the upstairs bar of a Cardiff pub downing a few pints when the landlord shouted: 'Christ, listen to this. Oh, Christ, they are all mad.' As Kinnock remembered it 20 years later, everyone 'crowded into the stillroom behind the bar to listen to the wireless. And we heard the news from Dallas. The drink went sour.'

A large number of British media celebrities were gathered in the ballroom of the Dorchester Hotel that evening for the annual awards ceremony of the Guild of Television Producers and Directors. They included comedians Eric Morecombe and Ernie Wise, who were to receive the light entertainment award; historian A. J. P. Taylor, then at the height of his fame as a television personality because of his unscripted lectures; reformed cynic Malcolm Muggeridge; playwright Harold Pinter, who was to get the best scriptwriter award for *The Birthday Party* and *The Lover*; actor of the year Alan Badel; interviewer Robin Day; and the cast of *That Was The Week That Was* and its producer Ned Sherrin — the doomed programme was to receive a special award.

Sherrin later recalled that he was standing in the entrance to the ballroom when he heard that Kennedy had been shot. He walked over to the table where the cast were sitting and told them the news, adding over-optimistically that the President's chances of survival were good. *TW3*'s 'chanteuse', Millicent Martin, recalled: 'We were stunned. We sat drinking coffee waiting to hear whether the awards evening... would continue. We

## The Kennedy parents

The President's mother and father were at their house at Hyannis Port when the news came through. Rose Kennedy was awoken from an afternoon nap by a maid, Dora Lawrence, shrieking hysterically: 'The President's been shot! The President's been shot!' The maid had heard the news on the kitchen radio.

By the time the President's mother emerged sleepily from her room, the staff were clustered around a television. Rose told them sharply to turn the set down, because it might wake her husband who was also resting. Then, before they could comply, she began to grasp what was happening. Bobby Kennedy confirmed the news with a phone call a few minutes later.

Edward and Eunice Kennedy arrived at Hyannis Port in the course of the afternoon (it was, incidentally, Edward Kennedy's wedding anniversary) to be with their parents, and they joined in a conspiracy with Rose to prevent Joseph Kennedy learning what had happened to his son. The President's father was in a weak condition after a stroke and, if not managed properly, the news could have killed him. Throughout that day the old man was kept away from the television or radio, Edward Kennedy even resorting to ripping the cord out of the back of a set to stop it being switched on.

Thus Joseph Kennedy was not told of his son's death until the following morning. He may have been the last person in the United States to hear the news.

**Kennedy's funeral: the President's coffin is loaded onto a caisson on 25 November 1963. *The Hulton-Deutsch Collection Ltd***

## A REVISED VERSION

It is often difficult to establish the truth of individual responses to the assassination. According to Andy Warhol's friend John Giorno, the pop artist's reaction was as emotional as any other American's. Giorno told Warhol's biographer Walter Bockris how, on hearing the news, he ran to Warhol's home:

'We sat on the couch watching the live TV coverage from Dallas. Then we started hugging, pressing our bodies together, and trembling. I started crying and Andy started crying. Hugging each other, weeping big fat tears and kissing... Andy kept saying, "I don't know what it means!" '

But Warhol's own later recollections were more cynical. He claimed that he had been 'thrilled having Kennedy as President; he was handsome, young, smart — but it didn't bother me that he was dead. What bothered me was the way television and radio were programming everybody to be so sad.'

waited and waited. Suddenly, people around were on their feet. Kennedy was dead.'

According to A. J. P. Taylor, 'all the television producers and leader writers left immediately. Someone, I think Malcolm Muggeridge, suggested that we should end the dinner immediately in honour of the dead President.' Taylor recalls countering with the argument that the guests still present 'would be aggrieved to be deprived of the flow of wit that they had expected'. He added cynically that there was no reason why they should break off the dinner 'in honour of some foreign ruler.'

Taylor's dryness about the President's death was not shared by many, but nevertheless the awards ceremony went ahead after a minute's respectful silence. Everyone went through the motions as they had intended, making the usual in-jokes and mouthing platitudinous eulogies of their colleagues

**Kennedy's funeral: heads of state from all over the world attended the funeral. Seen here following the coffin are Gen de Gaulle, Queen Frederika of Greece, King Baudouin of Belgium, and Emperor Haile Selassie of Ethiopia.** ***The Hulton-Deutsch Collection Ltd***

and the business in which they worked. But an atmosphere of unease and unreality hung over the proceedings. Robin Day later remembered: 'The witty after-dinner speeches seemed flat and inappropriate. If there was any topic of conversation apart from the tragedy, I did not hear it.'

The decision to continue as normal was also taken at theatres across the country. Actors heard the news as they were preparing for the evening's performance in their dressing rooms — the young Glenda Jackson, for example, was about to go on stage in *Alfie* at London's Duchess Theatre; Anthony Hopkins, an as yet little known actor, had to perform in Shaw's *Major Barbara* in Leicester. Most productions proceeded in an atmosphere of dazed numbness, both cast and audience feeling the entertainment to be unreal and inappropriate. Sir Peter Hall, however, remembered that evening's performance of *Richard III*, which he was directing at the Royal Shakespeare Theatre in Stratford, as heightened by the real-life tragedy: 'The artificial sense of evil on the stage seemed now to correspond with a sense of evil in our own lives. I never remember a blacker atmosphere in a theatre... Shakespeare's chronicle of blood and violence seemed unbearably true to human behaviour.'

Those in charge of the television networks had to make a tough decision. They could not run the Kennedy assassination effectively as a televisual news story. There were no pictures from Dallas, information was fragmentary and confused, and it would take time even to assemble leading politicians to make statements and pay homage to the dead President. Yet to go on broadcasting entertainment programmes might seem disrespectful.

Everyone could appreciate immediately that the assassination of Kennedy was not just the violent disappearance of a foreign head of state; this was a man whose death would touch the emotions and dampen the hopes of at least a substantial proportion of the British population. In the event, ITV decided to interrupt its popular medical soap opera *Emergency—Ward 10*, which had begun at 7.30, and after that commercial television broadcast only 'suitable' music interspersed with news bulletins. BBC, on the other hand, decided to press on with its scheduled

## CHICKENS COMING HOME TO ROOST

Among the most outspoken critics of President Kennedy had been the black Muslims of the Nation of Islam. Their leading activist, Malcolm X, had wittily but viciously referred to the three Kennedy brothers as 'the K. K. K.' — the acronym for the white racist Klu Klux Klan.

When Malcolm X heard the news of the President's assassination, he reportedly exclaimed: 'The old devil's dead!' In public, however, he was more cautious. When journalists gathered at Temple Seven in Harlem on the day of the assassination to hear Malcolm speak, they were hoping for some sensational quotes, but he restricted himself to a few guarded utterances on the lines of 'reaping what you have sown'.

To prevent politically counter-productive provocations to black Americans who were mourning Kennedy, Elijah Muhammad, head of the black separatist Nation of Islam, ordered all the movement's spokesmen to remain silent on the subject of the assassination. Nine days after the killing, however, on 1 December, Malcolm X could not resist speaking his mind. Asked what he thought of Kennedy's death, he commented that as a country boy 'chickens coming home to roost always made me glad; they never made me sad'. The implication of this quip — that white America had developed a culture of violence to oppress blacks, and now this violence had taken white America's own favorite son — was a point that many other commentators made at the same time. But coming from Malcolm X, and phrased in the way it was, the comment was widely resented as at best a flippant expression of disrespect, and at worst a glorying in the President's death.

The statement infuriated Elijah Muhammad and hastened the breach between Malcolm X and the Nation of Islam. Malcolm's break with the movement would eventually lead to his own assassination at the Audubon Ballroom in Harlem on 27 February 1965 — perhaps another example of chickens coming home to roost.

comedy programme, *Here's Harry*, at 7.45, and followed it with *Dr Finlay's Casebook*, although the next scheduled programme, *The Dick Van Dyke Show* was cancelled.

These decisions became a matter for violent controversy in the following days. Rivalry between ITV and BBC was at its most intense at this time, and both made what capital they could out of the issue. Well ahead in entertainment programmes, ITV was keen to establish its credentials as a serious and responsible network; its publicists hammered the BBC for showing trivial comedy while a nation mourned. The BBC, eager to shake off its image of auntyish propriety and dullness, pointed to the large audiences both *Here's Harry* and *Dr Finlay's Casebook* drew they reached fourth and sixth in the week's viewing

**After the funeral Kennedy's coffin was laid to rest in the Arlington Military Cemetery. All the visiting notables paid their last respects before leaving the graveside.**
***The Hulton-Deutsch Collection Ltd***

ratings, with more than double the audience they would have gathered on a normal Friday.

But the BBC could also claim that it was the network to which people turned when looking for serious information. When Kennedy's death was announced, 2.6 million people were watching BBC as against 7.2 million watching ITV; 15 minutes later, when news was occupying both channels, 4.9 million were watching BBC as against 6.1 million for ITV; by 8.55, when both channels were once again broadcasting simultaneous news programmes, BBC had the great majority of viewers, 8.5 million as against ITV's 2.4 million.

What did British people actually feel about all this? Certainly, some rang in to complain that their favourite television programmes were being disrupted; the fact that so many watched the BBC entertainment shows suggests they were less than prostrate with grief. Indeed, some people positively disliked Kennedy: author Adrian Gilbert, then a pupil at a Catholic primary school, remembers being delighted Kennedy was dead, because he was sick of hearing the President's Catholic virtues endlessly extolled by his teachers.

Yet the record of shock, sadness and anxiety is overwhelming. Enoch Powell, a Conservative MP canvassing that evening in his Wolverhampton constituency, was 'impressed by the apparent sincerity of the personal shock in those households'. Tessa Blackstone, now Master of Birkbeck College, London, was then a student living in Sutton; she had cooked a meal especially for her husband's birthday, but her husband was so distraught he could not eat. 'We just drank the wine I'd bought,' she recalled. 'It was a very bleak birthday celebration.' Denys Lasdun had just been chosen as architect for the new National Theatre, and had planned to celebrate with his wife and friends. Instead he and his wife had 'a solitary supper watching the television news in silence. All our pleasure and excitement turned to shock and foreboding.'

Even those who had disapproved of Kennedy's politics experienced strong emotions. George Melly stated: 'I remember a tremendous sense of doom. I was shocked, very shocked. That surprised me. I was not a great admirer.' Neil Kinnock and his friends had demonstrated against Kennedy at the time of the Cuban Missile Crisis. 'No one in my group wept for the President, ' Kinnock said, 'To us he was not a hero. But we were slumped and hushed. To us his killer was a devil.'

One example of the scale of public response to the assassination is clearly measurable. The US Embassy in London opened a book of tributes that people could queue up to sign, entering their personal messages of grief. By 10.30 p.m., when the Embassy closed its doors for the night, 42 pages of the book were full.

## Bad news for Fidel

It is ironic that at the very moment President Kennedy was shot, a CIA officer was briefing a Cuban, Rolando Cubela, on the possible use of a poisoned ballpoint pen to assassinate Kennedy's bitterest enemy, Fidel Castro. Not surprisingly, Castro was immediately suspected of having arranged Kennedy's death, especially when apparent links were discovered between Oswald and pro-Castro groups. On 7 September, the Cuban leader had explicitly threatened Kennedy, when he told a reporter: 'US leaders should think that if they are aiding terrorists' plans to eliminate Cuban leaders, they themselves will not be safe.'

On the afternoon of 22 November, Castro was being interviewed by a French journalist, Jean Daniel, who had also interviewed Kennedy a few days earlier. Daniel records that Castro's reaction to the news of the Kennedy assassination was: 'Es una mala noticia' — 'This is bad news.' According to Daniel, the Cuban leader showed genuine signs of shock and surprise.

Most investigators now believe that the supposed links between Oswald and the Castro regime or its supporters were largely or wholly fabricated by whoever killed Kennedy. It seems unlikely that the Cuban secret service could have carried out such an efficient operation in the United States, or have avoided bragging about it at a later date. And, although a personal vendetta cannot be ruled out, Castro had no real interest in seeing Kennedy replaced by Johnson or any other President.

World's Largest Evening Sale

# The Evening News and STAR

No. 25,460 LONDON MONDAY NOVEMBER 25 1963 PRICE 3d

## After The Assassination And The Anguish, The Vengeance And The Valediction, There Comes..

# TIME OF PEACE

### The Nine Miles Of People Stretching Over The World

From JOHN GOLD
WASHINGTON, Monday

THE final act in the tragedy unfolded in this mourning capital to-day.

Followed on foot by his young widow and the leaders of the world, the flag-draped coffin bearing President John Kennedy was borne from the White House to a funeral Mass at a Roman Catholic cathedral half a mile away.

Jacqueline Kennedy arrived at the Capitol a few minutes before the flag-draped coffin was carried out.

She was heavily veiled and her face could not be clearly seen.

With the President's two brothers, Mr. Robert Kennedy, the Attorney-General, and Senator Edward Kennedy, she walked slowly up the steps and into the Rotunda. There the three knelt for a minute at the side of the coffin.

### The Ancient Symbol

As they rose to leave, the Attorney-General grasped Mrs. Kennedy's hand in a tight clasp. They took a last lingering look before turning away.

Guards outside the door came to the salute as the casket was borne out the door and down the steps. An officer called "Attention." A salute was fired and a band broke into "Hail to the Chief."

The huge crowd in the Capitol Plaza was silent and stood almost motionless.

A U.S. Coast Guard Academy band gave four ruffles of muffled drums.

Outside the same six white horses harnessed to the same black gun carriage that brought the casket to the Capitol yesterday was waiting to receive the casket.

And again the riderless brown horse, the ancient military symbol of a fallen warrior, was behind the gun carriage. Reversed cavalry boots were in the stirrups and a sabre hung from the empty saddle.

The muffled beat of drums echoed as the military escort marched towards the White House.

The day was clear, crisp and beautiful.

All along the Avenue of Heroes from the Capitol to the White House it was as though Washington had lost its voice.

As the horse-drawn caisson passed, no one talked. The only sound from the throng was an occasional sob.

Walking behind the high-wheeled horse-drawn caisson immediately following Jacqueline Kennedy and members of the President's family were Prince Philip and Sir Alec Douglas-Home.

And General de Gaulle, West Germany's Chancellor Erhard, Russia's Anastas Mikoyan and a host of other representatives from both sides of the dividing curtain of Communism.

### Sad Flies The Flag

### The Children Get A Letter

Washington, Monday. – The first two letters Lyndon B. Johnson signed as President were to the two Kennedy children.

He said Caroline and John jr. they perhaps were too young to understand it all now.

### A FATHER WHO GRIEVES

### MRS K WEEPS

### FAREWELL
Love And Respect

Looking down on the thousands of mourners who stood for many hours in the freezing cold to move slowly past the coffin to pay their respects.

### John Asks For A Flag For Daddy

PRESIDENT KENNEDY'S son John is three to-day—too young to know what has happened. So during the sad ceremonies at the Capitol he was taken into a side office.

He saw a small United States flag and asked if he could have it. A Congressman gave it to him. And John asked: "Can I have another one for my Daddy?"

☆

John F. Kennedy, a tribute by Roland Thornton.

And now for the future —See Page EIGHT.

☆

The case against Harvey Oswald—See Page TWO.

☆

The stars to pay their TV tribute — See Page FIVE.

☆

Ruby asks for bail—See Page FIVE.

### THE PATH OF THE BULLET

### 'The Man To Whom All Looked With Confidence'

"WE mourn a world statesman to whose leadership in these critical but inspiring days all the peoples of the world, of whatever race, creed or colour, looked with confidence and hope."—

Mr. Macmillan in the Commons this afternoon. (See Page FIVE.)

Closing Prices Edition

YOUR WEATHER: SEE BACK PAGE

### PC INJURED AIDING BLIND WOMAN

### SMALL ADS. at a glance

Small wonder most people ring FLEet-street 5000

This leaves open the question: why was the response to the Kennedy assassination so intense in Britain and across the world? Enoch Powell suggested two reasons for the British reaction. One was the relative stability of life at that time, making the assassination seem more horrifying by contrast: 'We had not yet "supped full of horrors", nor seen either the collapse of public order in the late 1960s nor the saturation of the world with terrorism in the 1970s.' The second reason was the different relationship between Britain and the United States which prevailed then: 'The British man in the street still retained a sense of identification with the United States, which has been replaced by scepticism,

## OSWALD'S WEAPON

On 22 November, Deputy Sheriff Seymour Weitzman told reporters that the weapon found in the Book Depository building was a German Mauser. Later, this information was corrected and the rifle was identified as an Italian Mannlicher Carcano 1938, a weapon that could be traced to Oswald.

Some critics of the official view of the assassination have used this change as evidence that Oswald was framed. However, as the Mannlicher-Carcano is basically a modified Mauser, the main points of difference being the safety catch and the magazine, an innnocent confusion between the two weapons was perfectly possible.

The Mannlicher-Carcano, first manufactured in Turin in 1890, is a bolt-action rifle using a six-round ammunition clip. Much has been made of its poor quality and unfitness for precision sniping. It was the standard-issue Italian infantry rifle in World War 2 and has been described as 'the weapon that lost Italy the war'. But the Mannlicher-Carcano found in the Book Depository was the relatively rare 1938 model, the best variant of the rifle ever made and certainly an adequate weapon for a sniper.

Whether, on the other hand, an indifferent marksman such as Lee Harvey Oswald could have delivered even the three shots required by the official version of the assassination with the requisite speed and accuracy is very much open to doubt. It is technically possible to fire the rifle three times in just over five seconds, but this allows no time for re-aiming. If Oswald really was the sole assassin, then Kennedy's fatal head wound must have occurred by extraordinary ill fortune.

***Far left:*** **front page of the *Evening News* in London reported Kennedy's funeral: 'The final act in the tragedy unfolded in this capital today.' Unfortunately, for the Kennedy family, the 'Time of Peace' was to be marred by the murder in 1968 of Robert Kennedy and by the Chappaquiddick affair.**

***Left:*** **The alleged murder weapon was recovered from the Book Depository Building. Although initially described as a German Mauser, it was later confirmed as an Italian Mannlicher-Carcano 1938. The gun was capable of firing 6.5mm cartridges through its 21in barrel. The gun recovered from the Depository was fitted with a cheap telescopic sight.**

**On 2 December 1963 a memorial service for the assassinated President was held at St Paul's Cathedral in London. The huge crowds demonstrated the great popular reaction to the death of Kennedy. *The Hulton-Deutsch Collection Ltd***

alienation, even downright hostility.'

The image of Kennedy had worked upon the basic emotions of hope and fear. To some, this young glamorous president had come to represent the brighter, juster future to which they idealistically aspired; he was associated, understandably but wrongly, with a deep commitment to civil rights and freedom worldwide, as well as to vague but powerful intimations of a 'new dawn'. Cartoonist Ralph Steadman remembered feeling that with Kennedy's death 'part of the hope of the Sixties had been snuffed out'.

For more people, however, Kennedy represented security and leadership in a dangerous world. The confrontation with the Soviet Union over Berlin and the Cuban Missile Crisis had both generated deep anxieties and allayed them; many people, especially the less politically sophisticated, felt Kennedy was the man who could be trusted to keep their sleep free from the encroaching nuclear nightmares to which

## Harry meets Harold

Asked by the Observer, 20 years after the event, to recall what he was doing when news of the assassination came through, comedian Harry Worth remembered sitting in his dressing room in the BBC television studios in Manchester. The studio audience were already in their seats to watch his weekly comedy show, scheduled to be broadcast at 7.45. The decision was taken to go ahead, although a reference in the script to Khrushchev and Kennedy was cut.

'The audience enjoyed the show immensely', Worth recalled, 'and when it was over, it was the unenviable task of the producer to tell them the shocking news'. As the stunned audience, suddenly mirthless, filed out into the night, the studio was prepared for the leader of the opposition, Harold Wilson, who was being rushed to Manchester to pay tribute to Kennedy.

After Wilson's broadcast, the politician and the comedian had a memorable encounter. 'As Mr Wilson was leaving', Harry Worth narrates, 'I waited respectfully at the door, my raincoat over my arm. He stopped, looked at me and smiled. I smiled back, pleased at being recognised by such an important person when, to my surprise he said, "Is that my coat?" I said, "No". He said "Oh", and then he left.'

**In February 1965 an exhibition of Kennedy's belongings was put on display in London as part of a 15-city tour of Europe. Exhibits included the former President's desk. More than a year after his death Kennedy could still draw the crowds. *The Hulton-Deutsch Collection Ltd***

## PREMONITORY DREAM

In his autobiography *You've Had Your Time*, novelist Anthony Burgess describes a dream he had on 21 November 1963 in Tenerife, where he was spending the last night of a holiday.

Before falling asleep, he had been reading the Spanish epic *El Cid*. In his dream, he saw a crowded street in an American city. 'There was an automobile procession and a young leader stood up in his car to receive acclaim. "The Kid, the Kid!" the crowd cried. The name of his wife began with a jota. The American Cid was brutally murdered; his wife J... was in anguish...'

Burgess and his wife flew back to London on the evening of 22 November and arrived home to find that both television channels had ceased broadcasting programmes, although they had not shut down. Eventually, a news broadcast informed the novelist of Kennedy's assassination. 'I had to believe', he wrote, 'in the capacity of dreams to tear the veil of the future'.

all were prone. This may be why the reaction to Kennedy's death outside the United States was most extreme in West Germany, the most insecure of European countries in the nuclear confrontation — there was no equivalent in Britain to the sight journalist Neil Ascherson saw in Bonn, a woman 'screaming and crying in a dark street'.

On the night of 22 November, most British people went to bed more insecure and depressed than they had felt in the morning. However obscurely, they sensed that some kind of light had gone out in the world and was unlikely to be lit again.

By the time 22 November ended for the British, it was still only early evening in the United States. *New York Times* journalist Robert C. Doty described the scene in Manhattan: 'By nightfall, the normal quick Friday night pace had slowed as near to a halt as it ever comes... Most midtown legitimate and motion picture theatres, night clubs and dance halls closed their doors and darkened their marquees... As dusk came, automatic devices turned on the huge, gaudy signs that normally blot out the night in the Times Square area. Then, one by one, the lights blinked out, turning the great carnival strip into what was almost a mourning band on the city's sleeve.'

Elsewhere in New York the shutdown was less complete, but everywhere the atmosphere was muted and subdued. 'Bars were open,' Doty wrote, 'often with customers three deep, talking in hushed

## THE ODESSA FILE

'Everyone seems to remember with great clarity what they were doing on November 22nd, 1963, at the precise moment they heard President Kennedy was dead.' This, the opening sentence of Frederick Forsyth's bestseller *The Odessa File,* probably did as much as any other single source to popularise the idea that a universal 'flashbulb memory' existed for the instant of Kennedy's death.

Forsyth's novel went on to give a vivid reconstruction of reaction to the news 'on a chilly, sleet-swept night' in Hamburg, West Germany:

'... the music stopped in the middle of a bar and the voice of the announcer came through, taut with tension.

"Achtung, Achtung. Here is an announcement. President Kennedy is dead. I repeat, President Kennedy is dead."

'Miller... eased down on the brake pedal and swung into the right hand side of the road. He glanced up. Right down the long, broad, straight highway through Altona towards the center of Hamburg other drivers had heard the same broadcast and were pulling in to the side of the road as if driving and listening to the radio had suddenly become mutually exclusive, which in a way they had...

'The light music on the radio had stopped, replaced by the Funeral March, which was evidently all the disc jockey had to hand. At intervals he read further snippets of information straight off the teleprinter as they were brought in from the newsroom...

'The driver of the car ahead of Miller climbed out and walked back towards him... He wore a nylon fur-collared jacket. Miller wound down his window.

"You heard it?" asked the man, bending down to the window.

"Yeah," said Miller.

"Bloody fantastic," said the man. All over Hamburg, Europe, the world, people were walking up to complete strangers to discuss the event.'

tones, eyes glued to television sets that repeated the news over and over again.' Not everyone had tuned in to the significance of the events of the day, however: on 42nd Street, Doty observed a penny arcade where 'rifle shots snapped against moving targets and none of half a dozen marksmen seemed to think it was an odd way to pass the time.'

With all entertainment programmes and commercials banished from television screens, broadcasters leapt on any item of Kennedy-related news to fill the empty air-time — from the arrest of a man wearing a swastika apparently 'celebrating Kennedy's death' in Madison, Wisconsin, to the announcement that Cardinal Cushing would be celebrating the funeral Mass in Washington on Monday. Archive shots of Kennedy's life, solemn music, interviews with politicians, re-runs of the day's events in Dallas succeeded one another into the night. But despite the lack of incident, viewing figures did not fall away. Throughout the United States, people were bound to the minimal emotional comfort offered by television and its orchestration of collective mourning. One viewer, asked subsequently why he had watched until the network went off, answered: 'I kept waiting for something that would make me feel more hopeful or feel better about it. It never came, of course, but you're tied to the TV set in the hope that it would.'

By late in the evening, Dallas police headquarters had become the centre of media attention, as expectation mounted that Oswald would be charged with the assassination. Television, radio and newspapers had all drafted reporters and technicians into Dallas from all over the United States. The chaotic scenes at the police station have been admirably described by NBC journalist Tim Pettit, who had himself flown in from California:

'It was night when I arrived at Dallas police headquarters... At that moment, Lee Harvey Oswald was being led through a milling, shouting crowd of reporters and photographers. He was saying, "They're holding me because I was in the Soviet Union, The police won't let me have representation." Flashbulbs went off. Battery-powered floodlights glared. Microphones were thrust about like electronic bayonets. The eye of the live television camera peered into the confusion and transmitted the first images of Oswald, wearing a grubby white T-shirt...' Oswald was interrogated by the Dallas Homicide Bureau, and just before midnight Police Chief Jesse Curry emerged to announce that, as anticipated, the suspect was to be charged with the assassination of the President.

In the years ahead, Americans were to cling tenaciously to the notionof the lone crazed assassin, which allowed so many issues to be avoided. Tim Pettit, however, wondered if this was really the good news American TV viewers had been waiting for. 'As Oswald shuffled out into the midst of the Dallas media circus for photographs and interviews,'Pettit wrote 'it was obvious that there was no comfort at all in the idea of this strange man gunning down a President for no reason a sane individual could understand. Americans would spend years convincing themselves that that was indeed what had happened. But as the police officers and attorneys of Dallas preened themselves smugly for the cameras at the end of that appalling day, the sickness at the heart of America was plain for anyone to see.'

## Tributes

In the wake of the assassination, fulsome tribute was paid to Kennedy around the world. These are some examples of the statements of the famous and powerful:

Harold Macmillan, former prime Minister of Britain: 'President Kennedy was a man of the highest physical and moral courage, tested and proved in war and in peace. When things were difficult, almost desperate, he was both resourceful and resolute; and when things seemed a bit easier he displayed a boyish and infectious delight which was irresistible... We mourn for him and for his bereaved family, to whom we offer our respectful sympathy, and for the American people. And we mourn him — and this is perhaps the greatest tribute to Jack Kennedy's life and work — for ourselves, for what we and all the world have lost.'

Sir Winston Churchill, elder statesman: 'This monstrous act has taken from us a great statesman and a wise and valiant man. The loss to the United States and to the whole world is incalculable.'

Charles de Gaulle, President of France: 'President Kennedy died as a soldier, under fire, for his duty and in the service of his country. In the name of the French people, a friend at all times of the American people, I salute this great example and this great memory.'

Willy Brandt, Mayor of West Berlin: 'With the first citizen of the free world, Berlin lost its best friend.'

Richard M. Nixon, defeated Republican presidential candidate: 'Today, millions of people throughout the world are trying to find words adequate to express their grief and sympathy to his family. The greatest tribute we can pay to his memory is in our everyday lives to do everything we can to reduce the forces of hatred which drive men to do such terrible deeds.'

# 4

# AFTERMATH

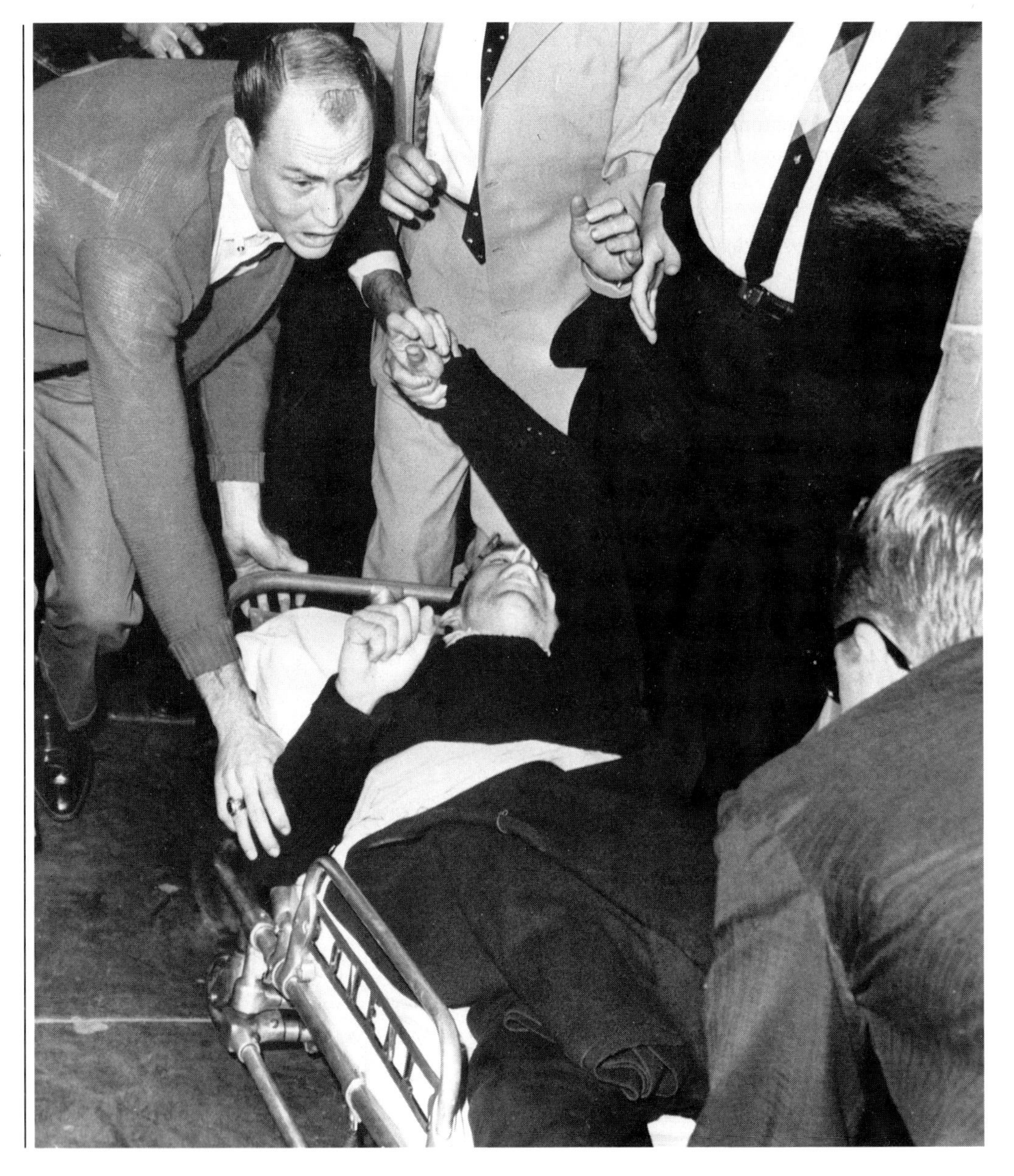

Two days after the death of the President, his alleged assassin, Lee Harvey Oswald, was also murdered. Shot at the Dallas Police and Court Building by nightclub owner Jack Ruby, Oswald was, ironically, to die two hours later in the same Parkland Hospital to which Kennedy had been taken on 22 November. *The Hulton-Deutsch Collection Ltd*

The drama of the three days after the assassination were enough to sate any addict of strong sensation. The killing of Lee Harvey Oswald by Dallas strip joint owner Jack Ruby in the basement of Dallas police headquarters in front of the television cameras on Sunday, 24 November, was succeeded the following day by the President's funeral, generally held to be the most moving public ceremony ever staged. Then a dazed public dragged themselves from their television sets and stumbled back into normality.

But, of course, the assassination would not go away. The American authorities, aided and abetted by the media, made a determined effort to sell the theory that Kennedy had been killed by a single crazed assassin. The Warren Commission set up by President Johnson to investigate the assassination was careful to come to the same conclusion. Although abroad many believed the killing had been the result of a conspiracy, in the United States those few people who had the temerity to question the official line were denounced as dangerous heretics. For example, in his 1967 book *Death of a President*, William Manchester becomes almost hysterical in his determination to finger Oswald as the lone assassin: 'Lee Oswald has been repeatedly identified [in this book] as the President's slayer. He is never "alleged" or "suspected" or "supposed" or "surmised"; he is the culprit... he is the right man; there is nothing provisional about it. The mark of Cain was upon him.'

Yet the doubts persisted and grew. Mark Lane wrote *Rush to Judgement* in 1966 and many others followed in his wake, until concocting alternative versions of the assassination plot became a national industry. Despite the release of secret files under the Freedom of Information Act in 1977, the mystery remains unsolved. But a quarter of a century after the event, an opinion poll showed that only 13 per cent of Americans believed the lone assassin theory; so there was no doubt at least that the

Daily Mirror

3d. Monday, November 25, 1963 No. 18,641

Kennedy drama—Oswald shot dead

AVENGER WITH A GUN

d, darts in front of Oswald. Detectives seem unaware of the drama

From TONY DELANO, Dallas, Texas, Sunday

LEE OSWALD, the man accused of assassinating President Kennedy, was himself shot dead today. He was shot down while he was being transferred from one jail to another.

And tonight 52-year-old Jack Ruby, a Dallas striptease club owner, was charged with killing Oswald.

Police said Ruby told them he took the law into his own hands because of "a deep sense of sympathy" for Mrs. Jacqueline Kennedy.

'I shot him for Jackie's sake'

He said he believed the dead President's widow should be spared the ordeal of Oswald's trial.

Soon after Oswald's death Captain Will Fritz, head of the Dallas Homicide Squad, declared: "The case of President Kennedy's assassination is now closed."

Jail

He said the police would still look for new evidence—but they were convinced they had built up a 100 per cent. case against 24-year-old Oswald.

The new shooting drama in Dallas, where Mr. Kennedy was killed on Friday, came while Oswald was being moved from the police jail in the City Hall to the county jail a mile away.

The transfer had been announced beforehand.

And millions of Americans saw Oswald on their TV sets as police led him into the City Hall's basement courtyard, where reporters waited to see him.

The accused man was surrounded by an armed guard of thirty detectives.

Other police were scattered around the basement.

Suddenly Ruby burst through the crowd of police and reporters surrounding Oswald.

He rammed his small revolver forward and pulled the trigger less than a foot away from his target.

Jack Ruby . . . "deep sympathy."

Oswald grabbed his stomach and slumped to the concrete floor. Immediately detectives jumped on Ruby.

There was pandemonium in the basement. Police picked up Oswald—and jammed themselves in a doorway as they tried to carry him into an office.

Medal

Then Ruby was hauled away and someone in the crowd shouted, "They ought to give the guy a medal."

An ambulance rushed up to take the place of the armoured car in which Oswald was to have been driven to the county jail.

And Oswald was taken to Parkland Hospital . . . where Mr. Kennedy died 25 minutes after he was shot.

The medical team that fought to save the President's life operated on Oswald. His heart stopped and surgeons massaged it. But he died from his

Continued on Back Page

**The front page of the *Daily Mirror* on Monday 25 November reported the second killing in Dallas. The paper reported that Will Fritz, head of the Dallas Homicide Squad, commented 'The case of President Kennedy's assassination is now closed'. How wrong he was!**

## POETIC TRIBUTE

Abraham Lincoln, the other most famous assassinated US President, had Walt Whitman to write his elegy: the result, 'When Lilacs Last in the Dooryard Bloom'd', is one of the most highly valued poems in American literature. Kennedy was not as fortunate in his poets. The most likely person to have produced a durable verse tribute would have been Robert Frost, who had read poetry at Kennedy's inauguration; but Frost had died earlier in 1963.

A young Kentucky poet, Wendell Berry, wrote an elegy entitled 'November Twenty-Six, Nineteen Hundred and Sixty Three' which attracted a lot of attention at the time with its stark imagery:

'We know the winter earth upon the body of the young president and the early dark falling; ...

'We know his name written in the black capital of his death, and the mourners standing in the rain, and the leaves falling; ...'

But this poem lacked staying power and Kennedy, in general, ended unsatisfactorily mourned in verse.

## Who Shot JFK?

That President Kennedy was *not* the victim of a lone assassin called Lee Harvey Oswald has been established beyond reasonable doubt. Even accepting the official theory that only three shots were needed to kill the President and wound Governor Connally, it is unlikely that the speed and accuracy of fire required could have been achieved by any single sniper armed with a bolt-action rifle, the Mannlicher-Carcano found in the Texas School Book Depository, let alone a relatively poor marksman like Oswald operating under great stress. It seems almost certain that, in fact, at least four shots were fired, and at least one of these from the 'grassy knoll' rather than the Book Depository. Whether he actively participated in the killing or not, Oswald was deliberately set up by others as a 'patsy' to take the fall for the crime, and he was shot to keep him quiet.

So who were the conspirators? Over the years of inquiry by official and unofficial investigators into the assassination, a wide variety of suspects have been listed. Originally suspicion fell upon Kennedy's communist enemies — either Castro or the Soviet Union. It was partly to squash rumours in this direction that the lone assassin theory was promoted so enthusiastically by the Johnson administration. Had it been discovered that international communism was behind the killing, the United States would have had no choice but to take retaliatory action, raising the spectre of nuclear war. If Castro were responsible, the US government would prefer not to know. In fact, communist conspiracy now looks the least likely of solutions to the mystery.

Some investigators have tried to tie the assassination to power centres within the US military-industrial complex. This is the thesis of Oliver Stone's movie *JFK*. The evidence for this hypothesis — apart from the known fact that Kennedy was distrusted and disliked by the CIA and the FBI — comes primarily from the supposed cover-up after the killing.

That almost everyone officially entrusted with investigating Kennedy's death failed to pursue fruitful lines of enquiry and avoided asking embarrassing questions is not open to doubt. This is not, however, necessarily evidence of conspiracy to murder. The Kennedy assassination was a can of worms, and a wide range of individuals from J. Edgar Hoover to the Dallas police department, and from the CIA chiefs to Bobby Kennedy himself, had their different reasons for keeping the lid on the can firmly shut. For example, Bobby Kennedy did not want his brother's connections with the mafia exposed; the CIA did not want to admit to their conspiracy with the mafia to assassinate Castro; Hoover did not want to reveal the range of the FBI's bugging operations; and so on. The lone assassin theory suited them all perfectly because it closed the whole episode, not because they were implicated in the assassination itself.

By far the most credible theory about the murder, as recognised by the House Select Committee on Assassinations in 1979, is that the hitmen were mafiosi. The mafia had the necessary skills, and they had plenty of motivation. The Kennedy crackdown on organized crime was hurting them badly; in their view this was also a double-cross, since they had helped in Kennedy's election to the presidency. And the mafia blamed Kennedy for the failure of the Bay of Pigs invasion in 1961, which they had supported because they wanted to overthrow Castro and recover their business interests in Cuba. Both Oswald and, more especially, Jack Ruby had mafia connections.

If one of the mafia bosses, such as Sam Giancana or Carlos Marcello, ordered the assassination, that does not exclude the possibility of the involvement of other elements hostile to Kennedy, such as individual CIA operatives who were in touch with mafia assassins, or corrupt members of the Dallas police force and the FBI, or Cuban exiles. The hostility to Kennedy in some sectors of American society, based on conservatism, racism, and anti-communist hysteria, created an atmosphere of complicity with the assassination that facilitated the killers' work and their escape from justice.

**Thirty years on, the controversy over who killed President Kennedy shows little sign of abating. Many of the accepted stories of the period have now been proved inaccurate, whilst new controversies have been sparked. Amongst the few certainties is that Jack Ruby, shown here, killed Lee Harvey Oswald, but much else of the story of that weekend in Dallas 30 years ago remains shrouded in confusion. *The Hulton-Deutsch Collection Ltd***

majority of Americans believed there *was* a mystery.

President Kennedy's posthumous reputation followed the spectacular trajectory of a ballistic missile. His glorification began soon after death, the retrospective reconstruction of the 'thousand days' in the White House as 'Camelot', a high chivalrous era of culture and heroism, political idealism and national glory. A wave of renamings swept the United States: Idlewild Airport became Kennedy Airport, Cape Canaveral became Cape Kennedy. An 'acre of English ground' at Runnymede, where King John had signed the Magna Carta in 1215, was dedicated to a Kennedy memorial.

The assassination of Bobby Kennedy on

5 June 1968, at a moment when it seemed he might follow his brother's path to the Presidency, marked the point when the trajectory of the Kennedy reputation began to fall. Jacqueline Kennedy's marriage to the Greek shipping magnate Aristotle Onassis in the same year ended America's love affair with the President's widow; the following year Edward Kennedy was involved in the Chappaquiddick scandal and lost any chance of succeeding to the popularity his two brothers had enjoyed. Then came the trashing of the Kennedy presidency, in revelation after revelation — of mafia links, womanizing, political error, connivance in assassination attempts on foreign leaders, naked ambition masquerading as idealism. To general agreement, Cape Kennedy went back to being Cape Canaveral.

Yet a large proportion of Americans of Kennedy's generation continued to guard his memory with love and awe. Twenty years after the President's death, author

## TRIBUTE FROM THE SATIRISTS

The *That Was The Week That Was* team created a special Kennedy tribute edition of the show in less than a day, for transmission on their Saturday evening slot in Britain. A recording of the show was flown to the United States and immediately broadcast there. It created such an impression that it was repeated many times, and even an album of the programme's soundtrack was released.

As a result of this success, an Americanized version of TW3, still fronted by David Frost, started up in the United States in 1964, almost as soon as the programme closed down for good in Britain. The series was not a success, but it is normally credited with sowing the seed for the Rowan and Martin Laugh-In which revitalized American entertainment television in the second half of the 1960s.

## WARHOL'S JACKIE

The most unlikely, but also the most effective, celebrant of the events of 22 November was Andy Warhol. Shortly after the assassination, he produced a silkscreen panel of images of Jackie Kennedy, entitled 'Jackie (The Week That Was)'. The title was, of course, a reference to the British satire show, whose Kennedy edition was repeatedly shown on US television. Warhol juxtaposed eight news photos taken before and after the assassination, including a relaxed, smiling Jackie in pillbox hat during the first part of the Dallas motorcade, a grief-stricken Jackie alongside Johnson during the swearing in of the new President, and a veiled Jackie at the funeral. Each of the images was reproduced twice, once the right way round and once reversed, and they were laid out in a strict grid of 16 squares. The effect is of a tribute to Jackie's dignity in suffering, a comment upon the transitory nature of happiness and success in the face of death, and a reflection upon the power of media images to engage and manipulate our emotions.

Kynaston McShine, of the Museum of Modern Art, New York, wrote of Warhol's *Jackie*: 'His multiplied images of those days offer the viewer an obsessive re-enactment, since the actual events had already been repeated *ad infinitum* on television; their inescapable repetition had itself become a part of everyone's consciousness of that time.'

Over the following five years Warhol produced uncounted variants on the Jackie images. She joined his range of obsessive icons of modern American life and death, along with Marilyn Monroe, Elizabeth Taylor, race riots, car crashes, Elvis Presley, electric chairs, and soup cans.

In 1968, he returned to the subject of the assassination with a portfolio of prints called 'Flash-November 22, 1963'. This used a whole range of images from the news coverage of the event, including pictures of Kennedy, the Book Depository with an arrow pointing to the fifth-floor window, and newspaper headlines. Shortly after completing this work, ironically Warhol was himself the victim of an attempted assassination.

**The dramatic scenes of the murder of Lee Harvey Oswald made the front page of the *Chicago Tribune*. In the left photograph, taken moments before the shooting, Oswald is being led out of the prison, whilst in the right hand illustration Kennedy's assassin is creased up in pain after Ruby's attack.**

Chicago Tribune

THE WORLD'S GREATEST NEWSPAPER

MONDAY, NOVEMBER 25, 1963

# ACCUSED ASSASSIN SLAIN

## *President's Body Lies in the Capitol*

Camera Story of Murder in Dallas Jail as Police Look On

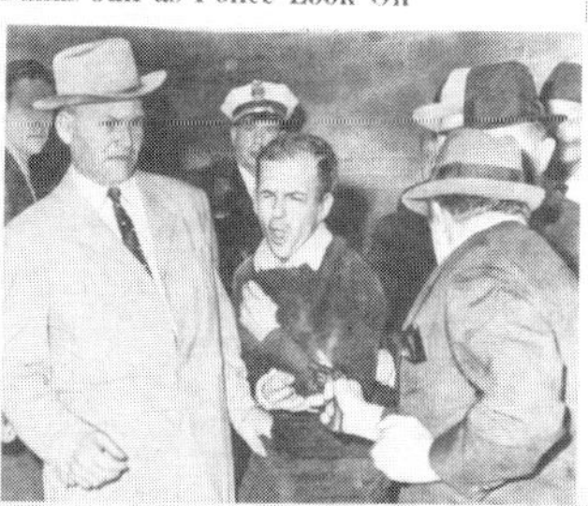

SCENE IN DALLAS POLICE BUILDING AS LEE HARVEY OSWALD IS APPROACHED BY JACK RUBY (LEFT PHOTO), WHO EXTENDS PISTOL AND FIRES (RIGHT)

### *Thousands File Thru Rotunda, View Bier*

America Pays its Ultimate Honor to Fallen Chief with Guns, Drums; Throngs Line Route

THE WEATHER

### WIDOW WILL LEAD MARCH TO CATHEDRAL

Mrs. Kennedy to Follow Coffin

### *Chicagoans to Mourn for Kennedy Today*

Catholic Schools Close

Park Buildings to Close

Jack Ruby

### FIND OSWALD PALM PRINTS ON SILL, GUN

Bare Evidence in Assassination

### *Oswald Shot in Jail in Custody of 60 Cops*

Night Club Owner, Ex-Chicagoan, Asserts He Did It 'to Spare Mrs. Kennedy Trial Agony'

*Taken Into Room Where Kennedy Died*

Theodore H. White wrote: 'The campaign of 1964, I realised, would be no fun. And no campaign since has been any fun, either. There was always hope, and wit, and grace, and purpose in Jack Kennedy's campaigns. We were all young then; and we, of our generation, have been no longer young since.'

The assassination heralded a disturbed and violent period in American history. The country plunged into the quagmire of war in Vietnam, and at home the struggle for equal rights for blacks developed into near civil war, with burning ghettoes and troops on the streets of American cities. Rather than standing as an isolated event, a monstrous departure from the norms of American life, the Kennedy assassination seemed to set a new standard of expectation that was then fulfilled with appalling predictability. The list of victims of assassination or attempted assassination lengthened through the years: Malcolm X, Martin Luther King Jr., Robert Kennedy, Andy Warhol, Ronald Reagan, John Lennon — so many bloody footprints on the trail of time since 22 November 1963.

***Above:*** **As part of Britain's tribute to the dead President a memorial was dedicated at Runnymede, close to the place where King John signed Magna Carta in 1215. It was unveiled in the presence of the Queen and the President's widow.** ***The Hulton-Deutsch Collection Ltd***

***Right:*** **The Kennedy Memorial at Runnymede.** ***The Hulton-Deutsch Collection Ltd***

***Left:*** **President Kennedy was finally laid to rest in the Arlington National Cemetery in Virginia. His death had a profound influence on the attitudes of a whole generation in the United States. Whilst the true story of the background to his murder may never be known he is assured of a prominent place in world history.** ***The Hulton-Deutsch Collection Ltd***